EYE
SCREAM
HENRY ROLLINS

2.13.61
P.O. BOX 1910 · LOS ANGELES ·
CALIFORNIA · 90078 · USA

Time & Inspiration:
Bajema, Shields, Vega, Selby, Mitch Bury of Adams Mass.

JOE COLE 4.10.61 - 12.19.91

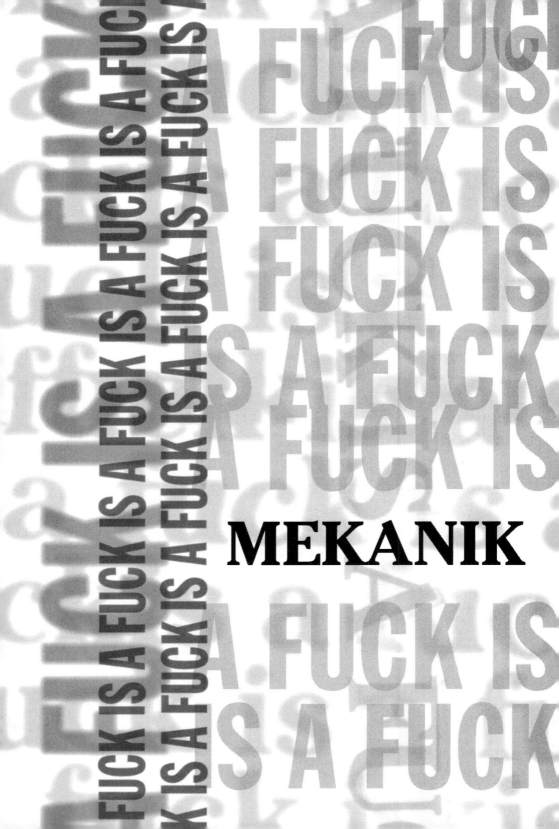

MEKANIK

Why do they call you the Mekanik? Because of the way I do things. Like the way in which I beat off. I employ smooth pulls, clean strokes, workman-like. I'm not here to enjoy myself. I don't feel the orgasm that I have. There's no expression on my face when it happens. No thoughts go through my head. I fantasize about empty space. I do everything mekanikally. I find the flaws in your structure and move in. I watch, listen and take down information mekanikally. I hate you piece by piece—mekanikally. Everything I do is methodical and premeditated. I never act on impulse. I don't believe in the idea that anything happens by chance. There's a reason for everything that happens. When you say you didn't mean to say something after it's come out of your mouth, you know you meant it. You're just too afraid to admit it. Before I take action, I consider everything you might do, anything you might say, any guilt or morality play that you might use on me or yourself. I am always several steps ahead of you. I am the Mekanik. I crush lies like a steel-toed boot crushes a rosebud or a child's skull. I watch you self-destruct. You mutilate each other with your emotional displays and superhuman dramas. You are your own worst enemy. I am devoid of emotion. Satisfaction is nonexistent in my world. I am the Mekanik. I am a pure survival species. Your bullshit means nothing to me. You hear all the shit I say. You think I made any of this up? No. I just vomit the words and attitudes that I have gotten from you and let you deal with yourselves. I didn't make up all the stupid lines men use on women so they can mate. That's all it is. It's mating. It's all you think about. You talk so much about, "making love", sexism and all this other shit. It's just mating, reproduction. You're just farm animals, more disgusting than most. I play you like a fucking deck of cards. You are a walking button pad. I can push them all. I can disgust you. I can say all the things that you want to but don't because you're afraid of someone finding out how you really are. You don't want anyone to label you with any of those bad little judgmental names. You have so many of them. You make them up because you live in fucked up cities and you don't have lives. Homophobe, sexist, racist, feminist, macho shithead, castrating bitch. You've got a ton of them. It's all about mating. Look at all the decoration that you put on an act that's as common as eating and sleeping. Enter the Mekanik. I'll give it to you until you can't take it anymore. Until you can't take yourself anymore. That's why they call me the Mekanik. Civilization has turned you into desperate animals in pain. The following is a sampling of your soundtrack.

Assault and flattery. He wouldn't stop staring at my breasts. He kept trying to talk to me and all the time he was just looking at my chest. I felt like I was getting molested standing right there in line at the bank. He was asking me all these stupid questions and he wasn't even listening to the answers. I excused myself and went home. I guess I'll go to the bank next week. Now I want to kill him. I'm used to getting stared at, but this was the worst. I actually was scared for a minute. The way he spoke was really creepy. He kept repeating the last few words of everything I would say, and he'd do it really slow. I can't believe I gave him my number. He just asked for it and before I thought of saying no, I had given it to him. I didn't want to be rude. He kept repeating it and saying, "Alright 392-9689. We'll get together, alright. Excellent."

I can't see how you got that gerbil up there. Hey you! Hey fat fuck, I'm talking to you. Hey pus gut! What the fuck are you packing in there? You must take some big shits you fat slug. I bet you can hardly find it to jerk it off. With all that fat, do you ever get fucked? Does anyone want to fuck you with all that fat on your bones? Your car's shocks probably hate your fat guts. Me and the boys should melt you down for lamp oil. Ok, your burger's ready. You want fries with that?

I like Styx, Boston, Kansas, all that shit. I threw up on the plane. I had never done that before. I didn't think I was going to and I wasn't ready for it. I vomited onto my legs and onto the floor. The flight attendant must have heard all the people yelling and seen all the shit they were throwing at me. She came over and started yelling at me really loud. "Why the fuck did you boot on yourself you piece of shit?" It was so embarrassing! While this was happening, the "fasten seatbelt" sign came on and the plane started to bounce and rock violently. A man who was sitting a few rows ahead of me told the flight attendant that the smell was making him sick and that he was going to puke himself if she didn't get rid of it. He said that he was going to beat the shit out of me when we landed. He kept looking back at me, pointing at me and hitting himself in the nose with his fist. I guess that's what he was going to do to me when we got off the plane. He told the flight attendant that this was his first vacation in years and I was ruining it with my puke. The flight attendant went away for a few minutes. She came back with a rag and spat on me and told me to clean it up. She said that the pilot had called down to the ground and there would be police to meet the plane and that I would be arrested and probably given the electric chair—Texas law and all.

Do that promo! I shoved three CDs up my ass and got them out of Tower Records. It hurt like hell but I did it. New Bolton, new Sting and the Best of Hagar. Totally painful. Definitely worth it.

Condoms from all ports. It seemed there was nothing I could do to make her like me. For weeks I tried. All the time, she was trying to be cool to me and trying to hint that she wasn't interested in me. I couldn't stop. Pretty soon I was no longer interested in her. But the fact that she didn't want me made me mad and more determined to try. It became a test of my will. Finally I broke her like a rancher breaks a horse. Now I can't get her off my back. She calls me all the time and she wants all this commitment out of me. I can't get into it because you know, I'm a swingin' kind of guy. Hey, whoa, yeah.

I collect samples of strangers' spit. She yelled at him, "You fucked her, you fucker!" He walked out of the room muttering to himself. "What the fuck did you say?" she yelled. "I said that I'm unhappy. I'm unhappy in this place." She started to cry and stamp her feet. "How dare you be unhappy!" she screamed. "Now I'm unhappy and upset," he said. She threw a shoe at him. It hit him in the lip and he started to bleed. "Now I'm unhappy, upset and bleeding." He walked into the kitchen, grabbed a small kitchen knife and stabbed her in the arm. They drove to the hospital. When they got out of there, they had found that a nuclear bomb had been dropped a few cities from their house making the neighborhood more dangerous than usual. They spent the next thirty years at a Best Western hotel down the road. They had three children who all grew up to be murderers in the great American tradition.

That's right. We do pizzas *and* brain surgery. Hold still! Her eyes. I can't stop thinking about her eyes. Her face, her arms, her breasts pressing against my chest. I can't get her out of my head.

Now I see why tigers eat their young. You know I was about to tell you that I loved you but I stopped right before it came out of my mouth and I'm so glad I did. *Love.* How hollow that word is. What a low gas mileage vehicle love is. What I feel for you is beyond words. Words fall short. Words get taken into a room and get fucked in the ass by one thousand lonely convicts before they get anywhere near what I feel for you. Words get their brains bashed out of their heads and get left in the woods to be eaten by bears so the cops will never find their bodies. I guess I'm really into you. I wish I could sing like that guy in Boston. They rock like fuck.

My name is Francis Sawyer, but everybody calls me Psycho. The teacher always told her not to stand up on the swing but she always did it anyway. I hated her guts because she always used to chase me home from school and pull my hair and try to kiss me and she was huge and she scared the shit out of me. Everything scared me back then. But anyway, one day at lunch she was doing her standing-on-the-swing stunt while the sound of the Jackson Five filled the air from a shitty close-n-play record player nearby. She was singing along with "ABC" when she fell off and ate it so hard that it makes me cringe just thinking about it. I swear she left half of her face on the asphalt. Who the hell knows what she looks like now. She was standing there crying and bleeding and we were all standing there looking at her like she was from another planet. I remember how we were all fascinated by all the blood and the pain she was in. The other boys were so taken by it that they forgot to beat me up all day.

My aura's bleeding again! I like to collect women. I like to get a lot of them into me all at the same time. I like to lie to them. It makes me feel good. I like it when they smile after I say something, knowing all the while that I don't care one bit about them. Sometimes it's all I can do not to break out laughing in their faces. There are buttons you can push. All people are mekanisms. I know where and when to push. I like to do it and watch them go. I don't know why I carry on this way. Maybe it's because I hate them so much. Maybe I'm trying to work out some damage from my past. All I can say is that I like what I do and I'm never going to stop and I'm never going to get caught. If they were small enough, I would hang them on my rear-view mirror or swing them from my keychain. They think the whole world revolves around them. They got another thing coming when they deal with me. Now that you and I are better acquainted, I'll tell you. I'm just proving a point that's all. When they try to give me the most common pile of shit, the pile that sends many men spiraling downward into their beer mugs, I just confuse the fuck out of them and then leave them to figure out why they're so fucked up. I have so many women to choose from in my stable. They think that I'll come crawling back to them on my knees telling them how much I miss them and how I can't live without them. All they ever hear about is how I did the same thing to all of their friends. When they pull their typical female bullshit, it's enough to make me want to kill them right on the spot. Do I do that? Hell no! I just say something really sly and stupid. You know, something *male*, and then I'm out the door and down the street to the next one's house. A few days later they will call up and ask how I'm doing and I'll tell them to fuck off and hang up on them right in the middle of a long laugh. I always tell them the truth right at the end. I tell them that I don't give a fuck about them because to me they're all the same. I think all of you are the same. Spineless pigs. You get what you deserve when you deal with me. If it takes me, the Mekanik, to set your ass straight, so be it. I'm here to get all I can for me and you and your stupid little fucked up emotions are nothing but junk food to me. That's all you are to me—human junk food. I chew you up and spit you out. At the end of it all, you'll like me, the Mekanik, because you'll see that I was the only one who told you the truth about what I thought. All your life you'll be surrounded by people telling you that they're your friend and that you can trust them. You can't. You can trust me though. I'll always tell you the real thing because I hate you all so much.

Hey! Free punches in the nose! Over here Bono! You smell like shit. Do you ever wash yourself at all? Christ, it's making me sick. It smells like something died between your legs. I can't believe you live with that every day. You know something, with a smell like that you're going to die alone. Damn, I nearly passed out. Could you tell your daughter that I'm here?

Man in the boat overboard. Please God, don't let this plane crash. I'll suck your dick if you'll let me live through this one, I swear. I'll do anything you want, you name it. You want some good shit? I got some stash that will get you so high, you'll forget who you are. I guess you already know that. I guess you could get better weed than I could being all powerful and shit. Look dude, please let get me off this one alive. If you do, I'll never play those shitty Limey faggot piece of shit dance records again. Please man.

Never do your friends with business. We are in the room. It's hot and I'm hungry. It's too late to go get something to eat. The room is dirty and it smells bad. The paint is peeling and the heater makes all the dirty clothes stink. She's yelling at me. She's wearing this old football jersey and an old pair of underwear that's full of holes. I sit and look at my hands. I can't make out what she's saying. She looks like a huge cow. I expect her to sprout wings and take flight. The room is getting smaller. Her squawking sounds are getting louder. I think that my head is going to explode. There's no place I can go. Everything that's cold, violent and evil awaits outside. I sit and breathe and stare at my hands. I want to be dead right now.

Zooropa? Are you fucking kidding me? What a shitty record! What a shitty band! Yahoo! How long are you people going to stand around and be insulted like this? Let's do a remake of *Day of the Jackal* We'll rename it *Day of the Jackass* and in the end you-know-who will get the bullet! I love art! I ran my tongue up and down her thighs. They were as smooth as glass, warm. Her flesh was taut over her muscles. I never wanted to stop. She pulled my head to her hips. Her fingers stroked the back of my neck. I heard her moan as she ground her herself into my face. She tasted good—the best.

American Psycho up on this motherfucker. She walks past the construction site every morning. Every morning the men yell shit at her. "Hey honey, sit on my face! Eatmydik! Hey beautiful, look over here. I've got something for you! Bend over, I'll drive! Take a ride on this iron pork horse!" She walks by this every morning and gets to the front door of the office building. By the time she gets out of the elevator and onto her floor, she has cooled herself down to where she can think straight and not rip the heads off any of the male employees who say hello as she passes. One morning she gets out of the bus and walks past the site. It's been months now and the men are several floors up and their taunts are getting bolder now that they're farther away. They start in like clockwork. There's a piercing scream. She looks up and sees a man falling from one of the beams. He lands with a dull thump on the ground a few feet in front of her. She steps over the body and goes to work like usual. You have to be ready for this kind of thing. Cities will kill you if you don't have the stomach for this kind of shit. A few years ago a man jumped off one of the highest buildings in Los Angeles. Some bank downtown. When he landed, he pretty much exploded. The father of a guy I know has his office right near where this guy hit and his window got splattered with blood and stuff. I imagine he kept right on working. Being in a city for years gets you used to this kind of thing. When they can blow your mind, they can control you. On the other hand, when you're numb to every-thing, then it's just as bad. Well, you can always eat me!

Right now I'm a famous actor but my dream is to some day become a waiter. I know this guy who got a second chance to live. He came pretty close to losing it. I mean losing the whole thing. He lived in an iron lung for a long time. By iron lung I mean he had a wife who took any opportunity she could find to step on the man's pride and soul. We all watched for years, not daring to get too close figuring it was none of our business. We all used to think about him and talk about his situation when he wasn't around. I mean this woman was really stabbing him. I used to watch her do this shit and I would be thinking to myself that the guy's dying inside. She's killing him. Have you ever seen a man's spirit starve and die? Have you ever seen a man get his chops busted so many times that he'll start doing it to himself even when he's miles away from the chops-buster? Sure, it happens all the time. You should have seen this guy. He'd be ready to deny himself his next breath sometimes. It was hard to watch. I mean you wanted to kick the guy in the ass and tell him snap out of it. So finally the shit hit the fan and he divorced this bloodless, soul killing psychopath. It took the man a while to get some blood back into his veins again. You know, you get leeched for that many years and you don't remember what real life is like. He came back to the real world where people breathe and laugh without having to be on their guard all the time from the hammering abuse of their "loved ones" and he changed. It's like he grew wings or something. He found out that all these people thought that he was really great and the only thing they couldn't understand was why he stayed with her for so long. He did because he's one of those guys who won't quit. I don't mean to be talking all tough and shit but I think that she fucked up big time. You know you rarely get a second chance at anything. Living is risky business. He got out of the iron lung. Wasn't easy. None of this shit is easy. So the only thing to do is to keep rising to the occasion and keep coming back. No matter what, absolutely. There can be no turning back and there can be no giving in because all of a sudden you're too old to get out of a bad situation. You have to ask yourself, "Who am I living for?" Next time you have some time to yourself, sit down and chew on that one for a while. By the way, this guy disappeared and came back as pure inspiration. Never quit. May your team win. Thanks.

Richard Simmons, coked out and chasing you around a hotel room screaming, "I want you!" over and over so loudly that

hotel security comes to check out the scene. There you are with a towel around your midsection trying to find the right words. Go ahead and shoot me then. With all of these people around, that makes a lot of sense. All these people staring at you and you're going to shoot me? Do you think that when the police come they're all going to dummy up and pretend that nothing happened? You think that you won't get caught? Are you that fucking stupid? They'll describe you down to the threads on your ass. Well I'm waiting, Mr. Big Man. Come on take me out. I'm getting bored already. Come on fuckhead, let's see what you got. I bet you haven't even got any bullets in—BANG!

A bit of the hair that dogged me. Tie me off sweetheart. Sure honey sweetie baby, I love to watch you vomit. Don't get any on my shoes. Oh fuck it, I'm so in love with you I even love your puke. You have the cutest drool I've ever seen. Better than your guitar player's any time. I think you're the raddest junkie-musician-poet-visionary I've ever shared a needle with. It would be an honor to get a disease from you. I have herpes scars from the best of them. Let's look for a new vein for you. The others are so flat. Wow, you've really been around! I love a man with experience.

Don Johnson's head in a bag. I think about them all the time. I guess you could call me obsessed. Women. I can't get enough. Am I a pervert? Call me anything you like, I don't care. I like the way they fit together. I like the way they move. I like the way they feel. I have a whole string of them. I like them for different reasons. Like the one I was with the other night. We were in bed and she asks me to talk dirty to her. I'm not into that kind of thing. She told me to tell her about her pussy, like how it tasted.

I told her it tasted great. She told me about how she gets herself off in the bathtub. She took my hand and pushed all of my fingers inside her hard. I thought she was going to hurt herself. Why am I telling you this? I have to tell someone. It's all I can think about. I see them on the street and I go wild. I want them all, all of the time. Have you ever met anyone like me? I have this theory that there are a lot of people just like me. Walking sex time bombs. I think I'm just healthy. Maybe too healthy. Have you and I met before? I don't mean you any harm. I just want to fuck you. It's not like I want to hurt you. I like the way you look. You look real good to me. Is that a crime? I get a lot of shit at my office for staring. I can't help it. I go to the restroom and beat off a few times a day to relieve the tension but it's no use. You must have seen me before. I'm a mailman. No wait, I'm a Senator. No, a minister, a convict, a fashion designer, a happily married woman! I'm everywhere. I am alive. I send letters and e-mail to the Mekanik Forum. The Mekanik understands me; he knows I'm not a freak. He knows I'm just trying to get by. Just remember that I'm everywhere and I'm not bad. I'm in a bad place but I'm not bad. You see me looking? I see you looking too! It's ok to look. You can't help it. It's ok to taste, you can't help it. Don't hurt anyone, that's not ok. More, more, more. I know why people do porno movies. I know why people watch them. I know why people need it all the time. It's not dirty. It's mekanikal. Don't be afraid.

Method achtung! I can't suck your cock anymore. It makes me think of an old boyfriend whom I really loved. I don't mean to offend you. I really like you but not like I like him. He was special. When you're in my mouth, I think of him and it makes me want to cry. You understand don't you? Are you guys gonna play "Runaway Train" tonight?

Cathological. Put your feelings in a box and send them home, son. It's either that or you'll crawl away from that girl, I swear. I know her well. She does things to you, makes you feel like you know her and then you find out that you don't know her at all. Sure man, have your fun and all but if I were you, I would keep a real good distance from her. Like don't love her or anything. If she finds out you love her, she'll make your life a living hell. I've seen her do things to men that would make you want to jump off the roof. Hey, you've got that glazed look...You love her don't you. Yeah buddy, you're in for a rough one. She'll put you through some changes yessir... If you need someone to talk to, I'll give my number. Don't worry, I won't play that "I told you so" type of shit. You can just call and I'll do the best I can for you.

Dear John, I'm only on crystal meth. Hello? Oh yeah. Hi. I was going to call you. I know it's been a few days. Three weeks? Wow, sorry. Where am I at with you? Ok, I'll here it goes. You don't do it for me anymore. I'm not trying to make you feel bad, I'm just telling the truth. I figure I owe you that much. I don't like it when you touch me. I don't want anyone to like me as much as you do. It trips me out. I mean you make me nervous with all the shit you say. Why can't you just shut up and fuck? I don't want to answer all the questions that you ask. Why do you want to know me? Just because we fuck doesn't mean anything really. It doesn't to me at least. To tell you the truth, you gross me out! Yeah you do. When you put your tongue in my mouth, it makes me sick. I understand that you had your hopes up about getting to know me and all that, but I don't play that game with anyone. Look, I have to go. I'm meeting some friends and we're going out so don't call here anymore ok? Ha ha, yeah, I'll miss you too. Bye.

Pin the tail on the daddy. I hit him to get his attention. I shot him to calm him down. I killed him to reason with him.

Nothing gets in between me and my Calvins. Oh fuck it. You got cash? I want to get out. She likes me too much. She wants to get too close too fast. She makes me want to get away. I see her coming and she's smiling and she wants to know what I'm into and she's all ears. I don't want to know that she wants to know so much about me. I don't want anyone wanting me that much. She makes me feel like she's trying to sell me a used car and wants me to sign on the dotted line before sundown. I don't like it when people like me. I'm shallow. That's it. Too scared of commitment and responsibility. Too scared to give up the ego trip I'm on. Is that it? Is that my problem? Am I an asshole? I want to pull the phone off the hook to get away from her. I can't handle people, never could. I am a shut-in. I was shut out for so long, it's hard to see.

Rent my ego to add excitement to any gathering! No one likes the taste better than I do. Only the crazy boys like the taste. No one likes it better than I do. I know what you like. I know what you need. I know how to do it right. I know how you like it. You want to feel good, don't you? Of course you do. I know how tired you are of these fucking idiot boys you always find yourself with. They're in such a hurry. You're frustrated with the incompetence of these grownup children. You've considered giving them up and just doing women instead. But you know what you want. You know what you like. I know too.

Love me, love my emotional baggage. I will never forget you. I can't get you out of my thoughts. Every morning when I wake up, I lie in bed and think of you. I think about what I would do if I saw you in a store or at a show. How I would try to look cool even though I was dying inside. I think of you all the time. You were never all that nice to me. You were one of the coldest people I've ever met. But still, you moved me more than anyone I've ever been with. I can still remember touching you. I couldn't believe it was happening. I couldn't help but tell you how I felt. It was like a dream that came true. An impossible dream. Any time I told you that I liked you, you would turn away and become quiet. I don't think you ever liked me. I think you just wanted someone to fuck you. You always wanted to fuck, but when we did, you always looked like you were watching TV. I was just the guy with the dick. I had a good time and all, but still, it hurts getting used like that. The thing that hurts the most is the fact that I lied to myself. I wanted things to be good so badly that I made up things to gloss over the bad parts. I know that sounds stupid, but that's exactly what I did. I actually believed it too. To want is a bad thing sometimes. It gets people hurt. It got me hurt. The world is a lonely place and people will go to great lengths to find someone whom they can be with. Someone who doesn't think that they're a creep. Just wanting to be able to talk to someone, that want will make you do some nasty things to yourself. I knew from early on that you were just getting what you needed. I thought that maybe at some point you might like me as well. I can't fool myself, I know that now. I don't remember trying harder than with you. I remember the last time you kissed me. It was like getting kissed by something that was dead. I remember your touch. It was cold.

Aim that fire extinguisher at my pants! I'm getting too inspired! I see her as I come into the restaurant. I look at her for a second or two. She looks at the chair next to her and then back at me. I walk to the other end of the room and sit in the corner.

A few minutes later I hear someone clearing their throat. I look up and she's standing there looking at me. She points to the chair opposite me and says, "May I..." I say, "Hey, get the fuck away from me." She looks mortified and starts to back away, but the shock is making her movements slow. If I had enough money, I would move to the desert and never see anyone again. Sometimes that's the only thought that keeps me going. I think that some day I'll get out of here and never have to see another human again. People bring me so much pain that I can't even bear to talk to them. When I order food at this place, I only point to what I want. The waitress thinks I'm mute. I'm just tired of talking. I've tried talking to you and your kind before. I see that I'm a million miles away. I didn't notice when she walked away.

Surgically implanted artificial tear ducts. I tell you what hurts. The part that screams non-stop yet escapes words. They rip me apart and destroy me from the inside. It's this thing that keeps me away from people. It's the thing that keeps me distant from women. No one will ever know me. I will never understand anyone. It's what makes me do all this crazy shit. It makes me think that I am an enemy of myself. I have to keep moving. That's all there is for me. I cannot find anything in anyone's eyes. It breaks my heart, but I can't stop. I can't stop my eyes from seeing. That's what makes me live on the road. I know that if I stopped, I would fall apart. I feel untranslatable. I have no control of words. I have to carry all these feelings inside like I'm carrying an alien in my guts. I'm a stranger to myself. I can't get in or out. The other night I was talking to this girl and right in the middle of a sentence I stopped talking. I knew there was no point in going on. She looked at me and asked if I was going to finish what I was saying. I told her no. Made the rest of the night strange. I got out of her car at a red light and walked home. I haven't spoken to her since. She must think I'm some kind of flake. I'm not. I just can't deal with it sometimes. All I can do is try to get the poison out of me. I try to do it. Sometimes I get a jump on it, but before I know it, I'm full up to the top and raging. It comes out too fast. All I can do is break shit and people think I'm just a garden-variety asshole. What a fool I was wasting my time talking to a girl as if she could understand me. What a joke. No one will ever know me.

Anxiety attacks! Collect 'em! Trade 'em with your friends!!! When she leaves, when she walks away, don't you feel like a piece of porcelain? If you breathe, you'll break. The nights get long. Endless long. Lifetime long. Hard to breathe. Hard to think when she leaves. You turn on yourself and try to tell yourself that it's not your heart that's breaking inside. You try to tell yourself that you're better off alone. Sounds fake coming out of your mouth. Sounds like a broken bell ringing. You don't have to be a genius to get the blues. It's like a cold that you can't shake. I get 'em, you get 'em. They make you want to die when they go away, when they leave you. Sometimes you get the blues when the blues leave you. You know they were the only thing that ever really told you the truth.

Flat against the irony board. Ok, let's see that dick of yours. What do you mean you don't want to pull it out? What's the matter? You think I've never seen a dick before? Let me tell you boy, this gal has really been around! What do you mean I make you feel uptight? Come on, pull it out. I want to see that thing! Oh wait a minute. I get it. You're gay, right? Why didn't you say so in the first place? I coulda kept on drinkin' this free booze! I'm a new age adult, I can handle it! You're not gay? Then what's the matter? You don't like to fuck? I know I have a loud voice! I don't care who's looking at us. What's the matter? You stuck up? I'm not good enough for you? Come on, kiss me right now. No, that's not herpes, it's a scar. A biker shoved a beer bottle halfway down my throat. Can you believe that shit? Come on, use your tongue! What do mean, *let you go*? Where the hell are you going to go? Look buddy, this plane doesn't land for another seven hours so you might as well get off your high horse!

Yes, I'd like something in a sucking chest wound please. Yeah that's right I'm the throwaway guy. I'm the guy you can use for a human doormat. It's no big deal, just my job. I live to swallow your abusive moments. I drink them in and hold them tight. There should always be someone there for you to shit on—that's me. I'm your man. I was working for this woman a little while ago. You know, she needed someone to bleed. Everyone needs some-one they can bleed. I'm just glad I could be there for her three years of need. I'm a throwaway guy—just use me up and throw me away. People like me are a dime-a-dozen. We are the ones that you forget about just as soon as it's over. You forget our names as they come out of our mouths. Somehow we make it back to the home base with smiles on our faces. You see, it's all we really know. You can treat us like shit and we'll be the only ones who will send you Christmas cards every year. We remember your birthday. You can call us at any time of the day or night and we'll listen endlessly. Your problem will be the only thing that con-cerns us. We have no lives, us throwaway guys. Our life is your life. We'll always tell you that we're glad that we can "still be friends." Even after you've sucked our blood, humiliated us in front of everyone and told lies about all the things that we did for you, making it look like we were just pathetic fools who should have been used anyway. Even then, we'll still extend you every courtesy possible. One thing you don't know. Every moment that you're making asses out of us and we're smiling at you, we are hating your guts. You think that all the stupid shit that's on your tiny mind is really important? What a laugh. I can barely keep from exploding in your face every time I see you do all that shit. We have the truth and all time in the world on our side. We watch and laugh and have a good old time. You think that we spend all of our time waiting for you to change your mind and take us back? We couldn't give a flying fuck about you and your insipid bullshit. All the time you think you're an object of desire, you'll find a throwaway guy like me to back you up. We'll back you up and make you think that you're more than the living scum that you really are. You can't live without us. If we weren't around to tell you how beautiful you were and make a big deal about your body and how fine you are, you would fall apart. You'd have nothing. Fact is that you need us more than we'll ever need you. May you eat yourself alive tonight. Leech off your own flesh. Drink your own blood. Dream deep baby.

I thought that was a dog around your neck! I hate to think of you. It brings me pain. You make me weak because you make me need. You make me want. Your very existence on this planet fills me with ugly fire that makes me want to shut myself off. You're so beautiful. I can't help but think of you all the time. That's how I destroy myself. That's how I know I hate myself. I love you and hate myself. The only time I feel alive is when I'm thinking of you and not wanting to exist. That makes me feel like there is a purpose to my life. I'm alive merely to torment myself for the remainder of my time here. I don't know if that's the way it's supposed to work but that's the way it works for me. Of all the women in my life, you're the one who makes me hate myself the most. I never knew the meaning of self-hatred until I met you. You've taken me to new heights of pain and humiliation. I don't know where you are or if you'll ever read this, but I want to thank you anyway. You have shown me parts of myself that I have never known. I never knew there was so much to hate about myself until I met you. Tonight is like a lot of nights I spend alone. I will think of you for a while, wondering what you're up to and what it was about me that made you leave. I'll wonder about who you're with now and wonder what he's got that I don't. I always think of you when I jerk off before I go to sleep. I think of how you left me and that gets me excited. You're the only thing in my life that made me feel alive. The fact that you left me shows me that I mattered, if even for a little while. You know, we all have little things that get us through life and as long as we just hurt ourselves then it's ok. Without self-loathing, I wouldn't exist. I will carry you in my heart until I finally destroy myself.

My dick is a macho shithead but the rest of me is a sensitive, caring and gentle guy. He liked to make friends with girls. They liked him because he did all the right things. He showed tenderness and sensitivity. He listened to them when they spoke. He was there for them when they needed him. They felt safe with him. He had a quiet confidence about himself that they could sense; he didn't have to try because he knew. They were drawn to him. He would let them get close and then intentionally confuse them with sex or lack of it. He would make them feel guilty but not understand why. He would ignore them and make them cry and then rebuild them. Their love for him would grow stronger than ever. He was an enigma to them. If he had pulled this shit at the beginning, they would have dropped him like a bad habit. It was the only way he could feel good around them. It was the only way he could feel good about himself. He was locked up in his head—a real case. He liked to watch them destroy themselves. He thought it was funny when they would allow their emotions to turn them into shit. The more they cried, the better he felt. It was the only way he could get back his self-respect that he had lost with women in the past. Revenge was more like it. It made him feel desirable. It was the only time he ever felt that way.

I hope you don't lose your job, Janet. I hope that you kissed the right asses and covered yours just right. I imagine at this point you're amazing at talking shit and I believe that you're always going to land on your feet. I was at a music seminar. My band, "Yeah, I Guess" had just played and this grungy, politically correct chick put some paper in my pocket. I thought it was an independent record company contract. I figured that's all it took. Like whoa, I'm signed. I mean I got what it takes. I got the grungy sweater, the greasy hair. I look like a scumbag. And man, I don't give a fuck. I really don't. I'm real. You know... grungy. But in a cool "save the rain forest" kind of way. Money won't change me. Below is what the paper said and below that is my witty/grungy reply. We made it into a song and it's cool because this time we made a ballad that's still got the grunge, but it's not like all of our other songs that sound the same. We don't want to be labeled. We don't want to dig ourselves into a hole. But still I think that... Oh, never mind. Read on.

> *Substantially our last meeting reflected in you a carnal interest that I in turn felt reflected in me. Bizarre rituals that are too metaphysical to be expressed on paper. Your animal-like ruthless-*

ness is thrust from your soul with every emotion
I've seen you exhibit on stage.

— Polly

What the fuck is that? Are you retarded? Thrust from my soul? What the fuck is that all about? Never mind, it doesn't matter. You'll be easy to fuck. You're stupid and it will be easy to lie to you and fuck you and make you think that I admire your brains and respect you. You'll like that, won't you? That's the last thing on your mind though. You just want to fuck me. I know what you want and I can deal with it. We'll see about all that carnality you've got in you. Yeah right. Fat chance, you fucking farm animal.

I lost the distributor for my label and now I'm going to drag all the bands that I signed into the egotistical hell that is my life as I vainly attempt so save face in the record industry. I have millions but you know what happens when a man gets his ego injured—war, rape, Rocky, little critic asswipes like the ones who write for pseudo-intellectual publications like the Village Voice and of course, books like this. Suck my mighty staff of life, you parasites! The way her neck comes out of her shirt. Her eyes, her neck, her nipples pressing insistently against the cloth. Her cheek bones, the way she smells. I start to sweat. I feel like killing ten pigs, cutting their ears off, putting a string through them and laying them at her feet. She's that good. I am an itchy monkey. Ung-ga!

I knew this girl who was picked up by Peter Frampton. He took her back to his place and proceeded to get wasted and passed out at his piano. She smoked out with his driver and the two of them split while old Pete was still out like a light. *Show you the way? Do I feel like you do?* Doubtful, you timid little vegan.

She wonders why I don't get mad at her when she's a total bitch in my face. Like when I talk to her on the phone and she gives me total shit or just says nothing. She'll call up the next day and apologize for the way she treated me and ask how I can put up with her when she acts like that. I tell her that it's cool and that I'm not mad. You know what? It's true. I'm not mad, not mad at all. I don't get mad at women. Do you know why I'm so at ease with the trauma and tension brought on by the union of the male and female? I'll tell you why. When that woman is on the phone giving me a line of incredible bullshit, enough to make me want to pull my hair out and jump out the window, I've got a woman in my shower getting ready to get in bed with me. I stay on the phone and let her get all of her hormonal and biomekanikal ya-ya's out with me. I'll use them against her later. The madder she gets, the nicer I am. While she's talking a heap of totally ridiculous bullshit, I know it's the better she'll fuck me later on in the week. Yes I go out with several women. What the fuck do you think I am, an idiot? Do you think I'm going to get all hung up on one woman and get all bent out of shape because things are going bad? Hell no! I'm partying in this life like Van Fucking Halen (back when they had Diamond Dave and not that right-wing narc moron they have now)! Let them pull all the attitudes they want, let them go wild. I don't take shit like that. You have to have more than one. Does a smart driver go down the road without a spare? Would I buy *The Best of Sting*? Life is too short to waste time with bullshit on the phone, long nights spent alone wondering where she is and who she's with. Let her do whatever the fuck she wants. Freedom! If you have a dozen options then you never have to worry about it. You never have to be jealous again. I think if we could hear tapes of some of the stupid shit we've said on the phone to the object of our desire, we would be so embarrassed we wouldn't be able to leave our rooms. The bottom line is I don't take shit from people. I work smarter not harder. I am the Mekanik. I know how all these things fit together. There has never been a female that has been able to make me lose my mind. If one goes on the blink, I just call up another. I'm not a sexist. See how fast you try to pin that one on me? I know... What about commitment? What about responsibility and maturity? Here's some rolling papers and my underwear. Have a smoke! You're just mad because you take shit and I don't. I get what I want easily while you struggle. I've got the whole thing in the palm of my hand. Fucking video games are harder than this!

I'd walk a mile for a mammal. My father kissing me. He runs his tongue up my throat, licks my lips and pushes it in slowly like a first date. He always tastes like cigars and beer. I suck his tongue trying to extract juice from it like I was trying to get milk from a teat. He pulls out and slaps me and tells me not to suck so hard. I must remember that. I will not suck so hard next time. He sticks it in again and I do it better. I suck his tongue softer. He doesn't hit me. He takes my hand and puts it on the hard part of his pants.

A backhand to the Brady Bunch. Mommy, come look! Daddy pointed a gun at his face and fired it! He won't get up. Mommy, he's funny come look!

Immolation is the highest form of flattery. I'm a sweaty hack and I'm in my room, drilling my eyes into the floor. All things that are second nature are turning into strangers every time I turn around. I'm losing myself in this room. I just had this thought. I thought of taking my gun and shooting all the people that are right in front of my window waiting for the bus. Something told me to stop. I don't know what it was. Yesterday things were different. I would have never taken out my gun to kill strangers on the street, but now I'm out of control and I don't know what I'm going to do. I don't know if I'm thinking or if I'm hearing another person's voice and believing it. Maybe someone's in this room and they're telling me to kill people. I don't even have a gun, I just wanted to see what you would think if I told you that I was going to waste all these people. I could do it if I wanted to. You know I could. It's not like I would feel anything for them. Do you think that flies masturbate? Have you ever caught a fly between the curtain and the windowpane and crushed it? If you listen closely, you can hear the fly scream. The sound of their bodies cracking makes me think that my brain is going to cave in. I think they masturbate. I always see them rubbing their front legs together and it makes me wonder.

Five bits paid for in cash by a sexier, more energetic version of Henny Youngman. I never hit her. That's the only thing I would do if I had to do it all over again.

A man came up to me the other day and said he hadn't had a bite in weeks. So you know what I did? I walked by him like he didn't even exist.

She laughed in my face. I told her all the things that I felt and she laughed me right out the door. I can still hear her laughing at me. Even when I'm alone, I can hear her laughing like a witch. I want to get on an all-night train ride and get the hell out of here. Affection is a disease. Don't get it, it'll wipe you out. It is disease. It is for weak fools. Not for me.

The landlord threw himself off the roof of the building. He hit the ground and the tenants laughed and cheered and threw garbage on his body

The next plane you get on will crash. I guarantee it. Go ahead, try it. If they don't get your ass this time, they'll get it next time. Thanks, you've been a wonderful bunch of stiffs... I mean... audience. I'll be back right after the break. Thanks for coming, or at least breathing hard and faking it. Get it? You, the one with the respirator, meet me in my room later.

Just be glad *you're* not in Poison, Warrant or Cinderella. Who do you think you are? You know you really have a big mouth. All these people I know think you suck. You know when you talk to them and you think you're telling them the real thing and they look at you like they're taking it all in? You know what happens as soon as you leave? They start talking shit about you and make fun of all the stupid stuff that you said. They can all do this great imitation of you. You know that girl you were talking to the other day? She thought you were such an asshole. You're so full of yourself. As we speak, she's telling her friends all the stupid shit you said and they're laughing their asses off. It's getting to the point where I think people are going to camp outside your house and wait for you to come out so they can laugh you off the street. It's too late for you to do anything about it. You blew it. Hell, even I think you're an asshole. I used to think that you were cool, but now I see that you're washed up. Forget it Jim. You're banned from the scene. You're history.

I skinned Edie Brickell alive in protest against what we're doing to the ozone layer. I remember he was telling me. He said to her, "I want to come in your mouth." What a limp dude. I can't even see how he got there in the first place. The guy seems so dead. He's staring at me and talking to me in that monotone dribble Californians seem to think gives them an air of cool aloofness when all it does is reveal how totally fucking shallow and brain-dead they are. They think they're so slick but they're the biggest losers ever—walking commercials. He's so boring when he talks, I struggle to stay awake, it's like trying to get through a Don Henley record. I could have gotten lunch between words. I just thought he was tired. I didn't know that he was a junkie. Anyway, he took a few days, but he told his sorry-ass story. He said, "I told her that I wanted to come in her mouth and she just looked at me like I'm looking at you right now, you know? Anyway, she did it and when I came, she froze for a minute and then she got up and went to the sink and spat out my come. That's it." I looked at him hoping that there was more to the story. I had been standing in front of this idiot for the better part of half a fucking hour and that's all he told me. He just stood there with his dumb-as-shit eyes and then said he had to go to band practice.

Olympic bedwetting team. I feel sorry for you girls. I can see why so many of you are into girls. I listen to guys and the bullshit that comes out of their mouths and it's pretty pathetic I must admit. I imagine it must really insult your intelligence. Sounds like they're still in grade school doesn't it? It's as if they never grew up. I can see you with your eyes glued to the ceiling as they pound away mindlessly. What a drag that must be. It's hilarious how much importance they put on your anatomy. It's as if they exist only to get in your pants, like you have some kind of life-saving device stashed in there. You know we're not all like that. Some of us have a grip on reality. You believe me, right?

Blues in my DNA. She was real mean, but she could get the happening drugs, let me tell you. I know what I'm talking about when it comes to drugs. I've been all over the world with that shit, man. That's right. I'm a big loudmouthed asshole who never gets all the ass kicking he deserves. I tell you man, she would do anything to get the shit. She would suck off a goddamn race horse if she thought it was holding. She had a mouth on her that wouldn't quit. If she was in a bad mood or if you pissed her off, she would give you so much shit you would wish that you had never been born. See that scar on my forehead? That's where she burned me with a lit cigarette! She was one wild bitch. You look so young, man, younger than she ever did. It's so hard to believe she was your daughter. She was real cool. You must be one swinging old man. Hey, do you know where I could score?

Anywhere the Marlboro Man hangs his hat is homo. I was in Tulsa. Winter. Got hungry. Went to a diner off the highway. I walked in. Typically half-frozen, watery-eyed and exhausted. No one looked up. The jukebox played. I sat down on a stool and waited for the lady. She came up cold and silent. I gave her my order telepathically. She turned away and came back with a cup of coffee. I drank and waited for the food-like substance. The jukebox played song after song. All about death! All things called out to me. The torn roar of the truck motors in the parking lot. The stench of the grease. The smell of my body and clothes, unwashed and fermenting. I turned to my left and I swear, I was looking right into the weather-beaten, wind scarred, dirt blasted face of Loneliness. His eyes were more bloodshot than mine. He brushed his greasy hair aside and tipped his cup and nodded. We sat there and drank the bad coffee, listened to the death rock. I swear I could hear the diner's heartbeat. I could hear its very life pulse! I thought, *I've hit bottom and this is the end of the line. I'm here and the sun is never going to come up and the clock is going to slow down and my heart is making my blood cold.* I listened again to the heartbeat of the diner. I knew I was in the guts of hell. It sounded metallic and mechanic. I swiveled on my stool and looked in the direction of the noise. The men's room door. The food-like substance came and worked its way down my throat. What a shitty heart. The men's room door. FLAP-FLAP. FLAP-FLAP. FLAP-FLAP.

Vanilla who? Oh yeah, that guy. Tell him I'm gone for the day and to leave the tape with you at the front desk. It wasn't as bad as all that. I mean he helped her have the kid. It wasn't as if he just left her in the street to have the damn thing by herself. I mean, what the fuck, he was into the bitch. It's not his fault she died while dropping the frog. When she started screaming, he didn't tell the bitch to shut the fuck up. I mean, you guys are trying to make it look like he was the bad guy here. I think he was alright. I would have told the bitch to go fuck herself, but you know me, I'm different than most people. I hate everyone, man. All that time inside you know. He didn't want to scare away the customers right, so he took her down to his car to have it. She had the kid in his back seat. I think that's pretty cool of him to let her have it there considering that he just had all that custom leather work done. That's true love right there! It's her fault that he freaked out when all that blood started falling out of her. She bled to death in the back of his car. He took her and the dead kid and dumped them both in the trash behind Pioneer Chicken on Western. It happens all the time. Don't worry about it, man. Don't go shooting your mouth off about the shit I just told you. It could get your ass killed around here. Know what I mean?

Suicide's illegal. Get married instead! She makes me feel impotent. Whenever I'm around her I feel like I don't exist. She makes me mad. I try to find the words but I can't. I want to lash out but I can't move. She makes me feel like I'm made out of wood. She turns my brain into wax. She pushes me around. I don't know how to say no. Every moment I spend with her, I lose a part of myself. I want to get out, but I can't see my life without her.

I get paid to be depressed. Life sucks! Eat me! Wah wah yeah hey now now! What do you mean, man?! I didn't steal shit! Who the fuck are you talkin' to? Get your hands offa me man! What you trying to do man, break my fuckin' arm? Come on man, give me a break. I won't do it again. I won't ever come into this store again, I swear man, just let me go. I swear on my mother's grave!

Peanut butter and spermicidal jelly sandwich. They have their rituals like any other married couple. At night, he goes to the bathroom before bed and masturbates. She does the same thing under the covers while he's in the bathroom. They come at the same time even though they're in different rooms. They have been married so long that they have perfect sex every time. After the lights go out, they sleep like real human beings.

At Christmas time, use condoms instead of stockings. When he puts it in my mouth, I want to throw up. I want to scream. I don't like the taste. I don't like any part of it. He makes me feel like I'm some kind of animal. I don't like his smell. I don't like the sound he makes when he puts it in me. That's how he shows me he hates me. I can tell. We can always tell.

If you weren't such a piece of shit, I could make you a star, baby. Don't take that the wrong way! Get a nose, cheek and boob job. Get the fat sucked out of your ass and your lips filled out and get back to me after you've healed and we'll do some more shots. I might be able to get you in the next Trixter video. I took him up to the roof and told him he could fly because I asked God to grant him a special aviator's license. Did you ever hear of something that stupid? He did it. He fell like a fucking stone. Pretty stupid, even for a guy into speed metal.

If I shot you in the face, would you believe that my love for you was real? The policeman's tongue in my mouth. I can taste it. His come is salty. A real man.

Detectives are pigs with ties. Don't trust the shitheads. A pig is a pig. I can make airplanes crash by praying just the right way. I can do it anytime I want.

You should stick a Habitrail up your ass and give those gerbils something do. That sick school yard feeling. Like when that guy is going to kick your ass. Even worse, when that girl is going to kick your ass. You can smell your own fear. You can feel it as an entity that fills you and makes your guts feel light. You can feel the panic go through you. The air takes on a strange metallic scent as it fills your lungs in short, spasmodic bursts. You feel like you're going to throw up right there. You feel like your body has nothing to it at all, like you're full of feathers. You're going to get beat up and there's nothing you can do about it. The hallways of the school take on a strange light and feel as you walk down to the exit door to go out on the lawn. It's as if you were never at the place before this moment. Your heart pounding in your ears. The guy behind you telling you that you're going to die but you know better. It's going to be much worse than death. He's going to beat you up. It's going to be scary. It's going to hurt and then you're going to have to live with it for the rest of the time you're at this place, which at this point is the rest of your life. Last week, you were one of the guys watching two other guys fight and you were glad because it was the most exciting thing that had happened for ages. You hoped it would be the one that people talked about for years afterwards. You were secretly overjoyed that they were fighting and not you. You looked around you—everyone was smiling and trying not to let others see. They were happy about it too. It was going to be great and you hoped no one would try to stop it. But this time it's different. Same faces, same glee and catcalls but now it's you who they're yelling at. People you talk to every day are yelling at you like they never met you. It's as if you didn't talk to that one guy in the green sweater half an hour ago in class. Now he's hoping for your nose to get broken. He wants to see your blood. One way or the other, they're going to be talking about you for a long time to come. If you win, you get all the respect you can handle. Even girls will talk to you. But if you lose, you'll be prime, blue-label laughing stock for them all. It's only September. You have a long way to go before the year is out. And you know you're going to lose. Good luck.

Don Dokken jumping up and down on his bed in a hotel room, playing air guitar and singing, "Breakin' the chains, breakin' the chains!" I hide under my bed when I hear my father come into the house. He comes home drunk. He comes into my room and touches me and makes me touch him back. He tells me I'm his favorite son even though I'm the only child. He kisses me. I can taste the liquor he's been drinking. If it's good stuff, I tilt my head back and catch the drops in my mouth. It used to make me sick but now I'm used to the taste and I like it.

Fuck Van Gogh. I'll send you both ears Mom! I asked her out and she said ok. I can't believe she said yes. I haven't done anything like that in years. It gets hard to talk to people, you know how it is. I wanted to meet her for so long but I didn't have the courage to go up to her and ask her what her name was. I would get up the nerve to call her at the place she works and I would pick up the phone and then I would freeze. I didn't want to make a fool out of myself again. I'd rather sit in my room alone for the rest of my life than make a fool out of myself by getting laughed at by a girl who doesn't want me around. It's too hard to take. Somehow all these people hear about it and they give you shit about it even though they've all been through it before themselves. They'll always tell you a story about what happened to them that makes your story seem like nothing. But when your face is burning and you have a lump in your throat, it sure doesn't feel like nothing. So she said yes. I meet up with her in a few hours. Now I feel sick. What am I going to say to her? I wish I never called her. I think I would have liked it better if I had just stayed home and watched television like I usually do on the weekends. I'm going to make a damn fool out of myself. I shouldn't have done it and now I'm going to get everything I deserve.

Liberally insulting Bono. It is my genetic imperative. You call that sucking dick, you stupid cow? That's supposed to get my rocks off? Are you kidding me? What kind of goddamn suck is that? What the fuck are you trying to do, blow up a fucking balloon? You're such a stupid bitch, you couldn't suck a cock if your fucked up life depended on it. What the fuck are you looking at? Oh shit, are you going to start crying? Oh, that breaks my fucking heart. You better shut up or I'll give you something to cry about. Now what are you doing? Are you getting frigid on me? Of all the fucking luck, of all the sluts out there in the world, I end up with the one that's so fucked up, she can't even suck a goddamned dick! Cut! Ok! That was great but this time with more feeling. Baby, you should cry more at the beginning of his dialog. Don't wait for him to call you a stupid bitch before you let the tears flow. You're doing great though, real passion. I could feel it! Ok everybody, back to one! Let's get the lights up. Time is money!

Like Socrates in hot pants. I can't talk to girls anymore. I get together with some nice girl and I think it's going to be different this time but it never is and it fucks me up. I'm lying in bed with a woman and nothing comes out of me when she asks me a simple question. I have all this shit flying around in my head. Sometimes I think I'm going to explode but when it comes out of me in the form of words, it is all fucked up and I wish I never said anything at all. When I met you, I thought it would be different somehow. I felt something with you that I have never felt before. When you first touched me, I wanted to cry. No, really. When you kissed me, it was like I had never been kissed before. I could get lost in your eyes. When I started talking to you, I couldn't stop. It all came falling out of me. I don't remember what I said. It felt like it happened so fast but I know it was hours. When I calmed down, I felt like a great weight had been lifted off my shoulders. But then I looked at you and my stomach started getting that frozen feeling like all the other times and I felt like I was a million miles away on some iceberg and I felt like some kind of fucking alien. I had to leave. I can't talk to anyone. I'm the only one here. Alone in my head. I have no one to talk to and I know that's for the best somehow. When I'm by myself, I know that I'm in the right place because as long as I'm alone, I'm not making a damn fool out of myself. I could kick myself for all the times I thought I could ever... Fuck it, I'm all alone.

Have Stallone and Bette Midler done a film together yet? I think about you all the time. I don't even know your name. I see you every day when I pass the store you work at. You never see me looking. I'm not the kind of person who has any of the cool lines to pick up girls with. You would probably laugh in my face if I went up to you and introduced myself. Maybe you would think that I was crazy, maybe you wouldn't. Perhaps you would see that I just want to meet you and learn your name. I don't have the guts to find out what you would do. I don't have a real grip on reality. I think that if I could talk to you then you would not think I was dangerous. I see the way they look at me. I tried to talk to a girl at the train station a few weeks ago. She ran away from me. People make me feel dangerous. I feel like killing them all the time. I have thought about killing you a few times. Stabbing you, you fucking stuck up bitch. What it would be like to stab you in your beautiful neck. How it would feel to kick you in the ribs as hard as I could. I think of holding your hand and talking to you. If I could write something romantic, I would leave it for you and I could be your secret admirer. You would meet me at the appointed place and time and I would shoot you in the stomach. Does that sound fucked up? Do you think you could love some- one like me?

Rattle and hum on it. That feels so fucking good! Take me to the Edge! The woman was seven and a half months pregnant. Hanged herself with an extension cord. Her twitching legs made it look like she was running in springtime with her hair on fire.

Would you like to come up to my flat and see the body parts in the freezer, I mean... my etchings? He looked so goddamn sexy with that gun in his mouth. It really brought out his cheekbones. Ooh, I get all tingly when I think about it. Let's change the subject!

Tango into Cash. Yo, his cock was like a 1972 Buick, right? It ripped my butt cheeks asunder!

Rocky I-V. It's so exciting when you come inside me!

As long as the guys on the ship don't find out... I guess I'll do it! Fellas, have you ever beat off and tasted your own semen? Do you know what it tastes like? Do you dare? Are you repulsed by your own bodily fluids? You should try it. You get all bent out of shape when she doesn't "swallow". You should at least see what she has to deal with. In the end you might agree with her, or even better, you might like the taste of it so much you'll ask her to spit it into your mouth when you're done. You could take turns with who gets to swallow! You might just want to keep it all to yourself. Do you think that if you eat your own come that you are now homo? Does that fuck with you? Could you tell your friends that you did this and not be afraid that they would think you were really fucked up? Are you uptight about your sexuality? Do you have a double standard? One for you and one for her? Are you a typical self-serving piece of shit? Wouldn't you like to rise above that lowly title and feel really good about yourself? Are you mad at me now because I exposed you for the nervous, bonding, shit talking boy that you are? Come on, be a real man! Swallow that stuff!

If you thought Rhinestone was bad, you should rent Oscar. Brutal. I was waiting at a bus stop. This guy yelled some shit at me from a car. I shot him and ran back home. That was four years ago. I think I'm safe now. I used to be real paranoid about the whole thing as you can expect. I used to have dreams about the pigs coming into my room and hauling me off to prison. Nothing ever happened. Looking back at it now I feel ok about it. I didn't know the guy so I really don't care. I used to think that there was something wrong with me because I didn't feel guilty about what I did. Now I see that there's nothing to feel guilty about at all. You do what you do and that's it. You only have to answer to yourself. You don't have to think about what anyone else thinks of you. It took me four years to come to that conclusion. You know everyone says that they don't care about what people think of them but you know that they do. I had to waste someone to figure out that no one matters to me except me. It makes life easy. The only thing that will fuck you up in life is other people's expectations. Don't waste your time with people. They'll slow you down every time. You know I'm right.

The last time I saw a mouth like that there was a hook in it. All that comes out of your mouth is bullshit. You need another nose job and some talent. You're not good looking enough to get through with your smile. You're see-through. You're just another fake-ass climber. You need a lot more than all that garbage that falls liberally from your mouth every time it opens. I saw your band play and you must be out of your mind to think that you're going to be able to take that out to the real world and have people like it. I can't wait for reality to smack you so hard the cum flies from your mouth.

My love is a one thousand snotty French poets puking black blood on your Cure CD collection.
I'm sorry. Do you forgive me?

You aren't sorry. You're just using me to shrug off your guilt. I'm not the one you should talk to about being forgiven. You have to forgive yourself. Asking to be forgiven is a waste of time. It's like asking the truth not to exist. Don't ask me to bandage wounds that you already healed yourself a long time ago. Now go away and leave me alone.

I owe you an explanation.

You don't owe me anything. You owe yourself. Like I said, don't use me as the way to get rid of your guilt. I deal with my actions. You deal with yours.

You're a bastard!

Why, because I won't let you out of the cage that you think you're in? You can get out anytime you want. Stop hating yourself on my time.

I wasn't straight forward with you so that's why I came over to your place, so I could talk to you. I really want to get it off my chest.

You weren't straightforward with yourself. How does that feel? You should have saved your gas money and talked to a wall. You're not talking to me. You're talking to yourself in front of me. Don't jerk off in my face.

Edie, what about that third album babe? 200 with an anchor!
What I felt for you was a combination of respect and affection.

There was a closeness I felt through intimate interaction. The affection part is all over with. All that remains is the respect. If I put my arms around you and told you that I missed you, I would be lying. You're alright with me and I wish you well. But you're not me and that makes you one of them and you can only get so close.

Your mouth is a gaping love hole. Shut it! Fear is an addiction, a disease. People become addicted to fear. Fear is a puppeteer. Fear is the monkey on the back of your soul. Its tongue is covered with shards of broken glass. It licks your brain to shreds.

Don't go to summer camp. Bury your parents in the backyard and have the place to yourself! You know I can't stop thinking about you. For the last two nights I've been dreaming about you. It's always the same dream—you don't want me. This morning I woke up and I swore it was real. I lay there for a while and thought about all the things that I had to do in the dream and how fucked up it was and it took me that long to figure out it was a dream. I thought I had it beat. I thought I had you out of my head for good. I must have slid back because now you're all I think about. I was so proud of myself. I was actually healing, but now I'm back in the pit of sharks teeth and razor blades. I would like to meet the man you're with now. I want to see if he comes from another planet or something because for the life of me I can't figure out what he has that I lack. You're a mystery to me. You always will be. I don't mean to bother you. It's the heat. It makes me go out of my head. When you get this, just throw it out.

Meat is murder, you fuckhead! Ok. I work for this guy and he scares the shit out of me. I hate him and I dream of killing him all the time. He scares the shit out of all the other employees too. At night I go home to a place that I hate. I can't wait to leave the hole so I can go back to the workplace. Do you believe this? I'm caught in between two walls of shit. I try to keep above it all and it's hard. A lot of people are in the same bind I'm in. They get into bad situations and it wears them down and they get into ruts and they develop bad habits. After a while, they lose their sense of pain and they go numb and they don't care about anything anymore. That's how we last all these years in these shitholes. We get numb and deal with it by not dealing with it. I get that way all the time because I'm going nowhere and I know it. It makes me sick and I don't know what to do about it. Sometimes the only thing I can think of doing that makes any sense is checking out. Just getting it over with and killing myself. I will never do that though. There will always be some television show that I won't be able to bear the thought of missing. There will be some ad that will make me want to live to see the light of day so I can go out and buy the damn thing. They keep me hanging on. Soon you get to the age where you cannot change and you get close-minded and full of shit. You will go unrecognized in the mirror one day and scare the hell out of yourself. You could always change but that takes too much guts. Too much for me anyway. I'm afraid of making an ass out of myself. I sympathize with you to a certain extent. I know what you're going through. I can only look after myself. I have too much hatred inside me to be able to deal with anyone else.

Treat me like you would treat your Mommy or a side of beef. I avoid big women—tall women. They scare the shit out of me. They make me feel like I have a small dick. I can imagine fucking one and being able to hear my dick rattle around in there. The sound of something disappearing, like a rock being thrown down a very deep well. This deep abyss, all consuming. I avoid them like the plague! Mostly they make me feel like I'm a small man. I like little women. When they can't wrap their hand around my arm then I know that I'm in charge. I feel good when I'm in charge.

The floor is my plate. I don't want to talk about it. It makes my head hurt when I think about it. I'm afraid what it would do to you. At night I dream about it. It positively consumes me. It's been such a long, hard road to recovery. It seems like it's taken me my whole life to get my life together. Ha ha, yes, I know that was funny. No, I really don't want to talk about it because when I do, I start seeing things. I'll start to see faces on your face and I might try to kill you. It wouldn't be the first time that would have happened. If I saw my father's face on your face, it would be all over for you. I didn't mean to scare you but I just want you to understand where I'm coming from. Sometimes I see films on the inside of my eyelids. I'll be trying to get to sleep and I'll start to see something that happened to me a long time ago that I thought I blocked out of my memory. I'm trying to get better. You see all the bandages on my head. They've been working pretty hard up in there trying to get my brain to work again. Sometimes I think they put other thoughts in there to keep me crazy. They can do that you know. You hear some of the things that come out of people's mouths around here and you'll agree with me. They must install thoughts in our minds to make us insane. I wish I could do the same to them. It's hard to stay awake for very long. They keep me pretty knocked out. Just talking to you makes me want to sleep for a long time. I feel so tired, so worn out....

I'd rather stab you than pay you. He didn't talk to people much. They made him feel too nervous. He was always ready to pay them. If anyone did him a favor, he would ask them how much money they wanted. Even if someone said hello in passing, he would hand them a dollar. He had no friends. He turned people off. They thought he was from another planet. The dollar thing tripped them out a little after a while too. But he had a point and they knew that he knew them well. Everybody wants a piece of the action and everyone has a price. No one wants to do anything for free, but they don't want to be called on it. He knew that the whole world ran on money and self-service. He never asked for favors. If he wanted something, he would offer someone money. "I'll give you a dollar if you tell me what the time is on your watch right now." That kind of thing was typical for him. He didn't talk to women much. He would bring up the topic of money and get into some pretty unforgettable "discussions" before having to run to avoid battery.

Found in three plastic bags on the 405 South. Hi baby. Sex God here! Whoa hey hey yeah! All things cool and heavy! Like last night, I was with the totally aw-sum chikk and we were kicking back getting ready to experience the wonder of my nature and she was telling me about how totally incredible and edible my body was! You know Mr. Natural, right? Hey! But even though she was heavily digging the fine machine that I am, I still had to think of you to get off! Hey baby, shake it all night long! You know I'm still thinkin' of ya! She was giving up the pretty non-happening head. You know a lot of air and teeth and it was going straight to nowhere! Like a lot of chixx! Hey, I'm used to the best. Whoa, what can I say! You really used to turn me on like super and low to the ground! Does the guy you do it with now do it as good as

I did? Whoa, like true confessions time! I mean like hey, I want to kill him! Like I told you, I was fucking this fat ugly skank bitch who was making noise like a fucking pig in heat and Babe, I thought of you cuz yur so fine! Remember all the names you had for me like "Needle Dick" and "Shithead"?! The best! I called up the radio station last night and had them dedicate ten REO Speedwagon songs to you! Party on, my wayward babe!!!!

Artists are so full of shit. It was hard not to think of you while I was riding on the bus today. The bus goes right by your house. I always try not to look but I always do. I wonder what you're doing in there. I wonder if I'll happen to see you on your way out or in. Usually I spend the rest of the ride home thinking about you. I know that's a joke to you. I wonder if you even remember me or any of the time we spent together. My problem is that I can't forget it. I see other women and I only think of you. You were the only one I ever met who meant anything to me. I didn't see your car today. I wondered where you were. Maybe at some guy's house. Not like it's any of my business where you go, but still I think of you with someone else and I can't stand it. There was a time when I would lie in bed every morning for a little while and think of you. I would think of things to say if I ever saw you on the street or if you called me on the phone. Sometimes, depending on the mood I was in, I would be friendly or abusive and sarcastic. Sometimes you would say stuff that made me want to laugh right in your face. When you used words incorrectly and you thought you were so slick, I managed to overlook it because I was so into you. Not a day goes by where I don't think of you. The bus ride makes it hard. Getting off in the fucked up neighborhood I live in makes it even worse. I always have to sneak up on my place to make sure I don't startle a burglar and get killed. It's no way to live. I miss you so much. You'll never know the pain I feel inside.

Maw, the punkers got into the fudge again! That untouchable feeling. After you've been through a rough thing with someone and somehow you managed to survive it and come out in one piece—whole, but harder for it. That untouchable feeling like no one is going to do that to you again and why don't they just try it and see how far it gets them. You might go as far as to get yourself into another relationship and test yourself by seeing how cold and *realistic* you can be. To see how far you can go without feeling something. Like some kind of drinking contest where you drink a gallon of gin to show that you're not drunk, that you can handle it, no perspiration involved. You can handle your emotions no problem. You can go almost all the way and pull out right before you start to feel. *What control you have.* You're so proud of yourself. You tell yourself that you're really doing it right now. It's a good thing that you grew up in time before you got yourself wrecked on another relationship. You laugh at all the things you did a month ago back in the old days, back before you got wise, before you saw the light. Before you got hip to the fact that the only way to enjoy the company of someone is to enjoy yourself on their time. To be open about being closed. To be honest with yourself about lying. To know that you're using someone's body to masturbate with instead of your own. To come to the realization that the only way not to get hurt is to hurt someone else and keep it that way. Somehow you make it alright. You have a better understanding of yourself now and you've learned that it's ok to feel good even if it's at someone else's expense. It's ok because you're your own best friend. No one loves you like you do. You gotta look out for Number One.

Because that's the only one who matters—you. You tell yourself that you've been through the ringer and you're smarter, stronger and tougher now because of all your trials and troubles. The reality is that you're meaner, more petty and cruel than you ever were and it doesn't matter who the next person in your life is. They're not going to get away with what the last one did. And why not? Because you will get away with it first.

No, it's not a fur cap on my head. It's my mother's scalp! I call them up to see how they're doing. You know, like, "Hi baby, I know that you and I are no longer glued together by our bodily secretions but I just wanted to say hello and see what's happening." I like to do that because after I love them and leave them. I know they can't get with someone else for a long time and that's how I keep them, even after I've cut them loose. It's a game that I like to play, it's a thing that I do. Don't get me wrong and think that I don't like women. I love them. That's why I end up being with so many. I like it best when they tell me that they're doing fine but their voice gives them away. It's so cute. I hear them trying to be strong and independent, all the while they have been thinking of me the whole time. Meanwhile, I have been screwing her best friend and that girl will never tell because she has too much to lose. It's always good for a few more mercy fucks, you know what I mean? You get enough of these going and you will never be without company five nights a week. Best thing is that a woman you have already been with will fuck the daylights out of you to get you back. It's the post-relationship sex that you have to get. It's by far the best. The thing that pisses me off though was when they tell me that they've found someone else and they're the happiest they've ever been. I get jealous as hell. I want to have enough control so I can *not* see them when I want to. I play them like a puppet show. Hold on, the phone is ringing. It'll only take a minute. Hello baby, I was just talking about you! Yeah it's been a long time. What? Not since me? You must be going out of your mind! Sure what time? Sounds good. See you tonight.... You see what I mean? Haven't talked to her in four months! I tell you my man, all you have to do is build up a stable and then you're really in for the time of your life!

Fedex me your brain. Fax me your soul. You see it now. You're a shadow of yourself. They got you. They chewed you up and spat you out. You see it now. They put you on drugs and they drove you up the wall and then they let you drop. They left the room and you had only yourself to blame. It's too late—the damage is done. The sun is setting. The men are rolling up the carpet and sweeping the floor. All the secrets have been re-vealed. All the times that you thought you were giving yourself, you see now that you were just being used. You believed some-thing in your sleep and you took it for truth and now you have life's cancer. For who? For what? For nothing. No one's anything. You see it now. You see that it's too late.

Pig with a cumcatcher mustache. I always thought you were a fake. I see you differently now. You don't know who you are. I thought you were full of shit but now I see that you don't even have that much together. Here I was getting all wrapped up in what you were saying when you didn't know what you were talking about. I used to get so frustrated trying to figure out all the stupid things you were saying because I thought they actu-ally meant something. I used to think that I was an idiot! I used to lose sleep trying to find ways to get close to you. Now I see that there was nothing to get close to. Thinking back on it now, I filled in a lot of the blanks. All the things I took for fake, I just smoothed over in hopes of you dropping it and getting real. At first, I was sad that it never happened. Now I see you for what you are. I wish you all the luck. You'll need it. I think you're going to find a lot of hardship and pain. You're a beautiful shell. I was attracted to the shell and what I thought it might hold. I made a mistake. I make them all the time. I thought you were a fake, but now I see that your artificiality is real.

Party in my trunk. Pulling away from you, I think I'll be feeling a lot better in the next few weeks. I'll be far away from you. You're strong; you had me in close. It was hard to see the destruction that you were putting to me. It was so overwhelming that I got lost in it. I got lost in your world. I forgot myself. I didn't know who I was anymore. Maybe I thought I was you. I was losing myself more with every breath. You told me that you loved me. I think you did that because you wanted to watch all the blood come out. Love pulled me in and tried to kill me. No one ever told me that they loved me before. It made me feel like I was getting crushed. I had to get away from you. I'm learning how to breathe again. It's good to be away from you. It's good to be alive. I thank myself for crawling away.

Saddle up Grace Jones, I want to feel the wind in my hair. It was so easy—the way all those guys took you. The way he did it to you over and over? You fell for it every time. So hungry for the real thing that you jumped at any piece of garbage who smiled at you. It's hard to take you seriously sometimes with all your tales of woe and heartbreak. I think you got good at finding guys who you know would hurt you. I don't think you would like me. I wouldn't take you and crush you like that. You would probably call me a wimp and go running for a real man—one who will smack the shit out of you and make you feel like a real woman.

You need the pain and humiliation to make you feel like you're worth something. It gives you the chance to feel like you're part of something. I think that everyone needs that to a certain extent. Idiots take it too far. Look at you getting beaten badly every six weeks or so and telling me that life's not too bad.

I'm not the bastard you're paying me to be. I immediately liked you a lot less when I got your clothes off. I guess I'm too hung up on appearances. I have heard that if you really like someone then it doesn't matter what they look like. You know, I've always thought that was a pile of bullshit. It's something that fucked up looking people made up so they could get some. Anyway, back to you and your body. The cellulite on your ass and the stretch marks on your tits make it hard to go on. This will be an act of mercenary strength on my part. Maybe next time you can keep your clothes on and I can just hike up your skirt and I won't have to look. I think you're really cool and all but I can't take it when you try to stick your tongue in my mouth. I think you'll have to start finding more desperate guys to fuck. I know you don't listen to the things I say. You think I'm a moron and you only like me for my good looks. At least we don't have to beat around the bush and talk about our deep emotions and how we feel about each other. I'll let you suck my cock and that's it. I couldn't face the rest. If I smell you, I'll lose my erection. You understand, don't you? You've seen yourself in the mirror right? Pretty disgusting. If I looked like you, I would kill myself but that's me. Whatever.

Welcome to the salon. I'm going to do something really insane to your hair. I know it sounds pathetic but would you touch me? I need someone to touch me. It's been so long. Don't get me wrong, I'm not looking for some kind of mercy fuck. I like you. I feel ok when I'm around you. It's so hard to be around people, they're so fucked up. I know all this sounds strange to you. You probably think I'm some kind of idiot, I'm not. It's just that it's so hard to be around them. They can make me feel so crummy about myself that I never want to come out of my room again. It doesn't even matter if you like me or not. I don't mind. It felt good just being able to say that out loud. I feel like a great weight has been lifted off my shoulders.

I liked you better when your nose was bigger, your lips were thinner and your breasts were smaller. I wanted to tell you. I don't want to call you on the phone. I hate those damn things. They make me feel like an idiot. I'm writing you instead. I know if I wait another day, I won't even be able to do that. Well, here goes... You are the first person that I ever wanted to punch in the mouth. I don't guess you to want to hear that but it's the truth. I think you're a stupid piece of shit. You buy me food and then you want to fuck me. I have to leave to go to work and you get all mad at me and tell me that I'm not paying attention to you. You want me more than I'll ever need you. You're all the same at the end of the day. You're self-centered and boring. You like it when people will stop their lives for you. You need to feel like you're so special that someone could lose their mind over you. You must think you are the end of the rainbow. You're not. Humans are a dime-a-dozen. You're so common, it's so pathetic to think of you alone in your room waiting to trap another person in your web of bullshit. You hate yourself. Leave the rest of us out of it.

I only do it to my shrink... on the couch with the lights on full. When I saw you waddle past me with your two kids, I felt sorry for your husband. Imagine him trying to get excited over that wide ass of yours. I bet he feels like a man whose life has ended way too early. Well, shut my mouth! Who the hell do I think am talking like that? I have no right! Maybe your husband is a fat piece of shit just like you and he doesn't notice. Maybe you really turn him on. Maybe that ten mile wide ass of yours gets him going. Maybe he thinks that's the best thing he's ever seen. Come on, let's not kid ourselves here. I could be really out of line. I'm already politically incorrect so I might as well go the rest of the way. I'm just a shit talking fool who thinks moms with big mom asses and loud kids make for just about the most tragic blues situation ever—like the total downfall of civilization. Now you really got me worked up, you fucking hog! I can see you strapped down on a table with babies shooting out of you and smashing against the facing wall. The gyno is in a yellow rainsuit with matching hat. He's wearing black leather boots and has pierced nipples. He's jumping up and down on the little tykes and there's blood and guts a plenty! Ok, that was just a joke, the whole thing was just a joke. I think you look great, really fine. In fact, I think that your husband's a really lucky guy. Now why don't you stop breeding for a second, as if there's really enough food and jobs for all these people.

Roller-skate on my heart, Baby. I fill them with lies! All the time I fill them with lies. When I fuck them and tell them I love them, I am lying. Oh how I lie! I am a pathological liar. It's the only logical path I know. I am a disease. I get under their skin and into their bloodstream. When I have them where I want them, I fill them with lies. Every word I say to them is a lie. I lie with total passion and sincerity, heart and soul. I love to lie! I see their eyes light up when I pass the false fire to them. They swear it's real. It's the only time I feel like I'm in control. Yes dear, I miss you already! My world is a better place with you in it! I love you! WHAT A BEAUTIFUL STACK OF LIES!!! I cover women with filth.

I turn women into shit. I can do it to any woman. I can do it to your mother. I can do it to your sister, any female. I'm that good. At this point I should introduce myself. My name is Love. I have a partner named Lust. We work as a double act and we never lose. We never sleep. Why the hell should we? We have to be out there putting ourselves in the middle of every thought and act on the planet. We have a sucker we set up and use like a home appliance. His name is Desire. We let him think that he's our right hand man. He's a stupid as can be, blind all the way. He injects the serum that destroys truth. I am the seeing eye. I start all wars. I spin you pigs around until blood flies from your assholes. Hail!

I know... I'll call myself Sting too! I don't know what it is about me. I've tried to figure it out for years.... about why I'm the Mekanik. That's who I am you know. I picked up this girl last night just to keep my chops you know. I played her like a game of pool. I did it just to have some fun. Almost piss her off and then at the last minute reel her in like a fish. It's easy. You're all easy. I play them like a guitar. I don't even care about the sex. I just like to push the buttons. It's to the point to where I can't help myself. I see a mark and I just got to take them out. I push buttons that I don't even want to push just to see if I can do it. They all sound the same after awhile. The same stories—the same bullshit. They act the same when I push the buttons. Just a toy I play with to pass the time. You think it's amazing that some rock band can fill up a stadium and do it every night all over the world? You're impressed with that? You're just another sucker. That shit's nothing. Say the right things and it's money in the bank. A real pro can play it off like it's nothing. I take you for all you got. I play you against your own bullshit. I can get the skirt off a woman in a painting. You're all easy. You're mine.

***Men who don't want to be penetrated are lightweight and are in fear of intensity?* Village feminists are hilarious. You should put on a show sometime!** I tried to feel something. I loved her and she loved me. I don't know what happened. Everything was going well and then all of a sudden, I got cold like there was a stranger next to me. I tried to get rid of the feeling but it swallowed me. She asked me what my problem was and how could she help. She was right next to me and it sounded like she was talking to me from another planet. I almost forgot her name! I still don't understand it. I was in love with her and then in a flash I couldn't think of a single reason that I should be with her. I left her that night and haven't spoken to her since.

Shut up, get a life and stop getting your genitals pierced. We're not paying attention. Here I come with a knife. Are you ready? Here I come. I'm coming with a gun. Are your ready for me? Huh? Are you ready? Here I come. I'm coming with a gun and I'm gonna shoot you in the face! Hey, I'm talking to you! I'm a killer and I'm gonna kill you! Your morality is making you hesitate. Thou shalt not kill? Thou is going to get killed! Will you survive me or will your upbringing be your undoing?

Critical acclaim? Critical backlash? I'm supposed to care what a bunch of frustrated novelists and closet rockstar wannabes think about anything? You'll never catch up to me you frustrated little temps! I didn't want to hurt her. I said that in court. I said that I didn't hate her or anything. It was the way she would laugh. She would laugh at everything I said. It was like I was some kind of comedian. Do I look funny? Right. It got to me. I'd ask her what her fucking problem was and she'd laugh. All the time laughing. Not like she would ever open up and really let one out, but laughing like you had fucked up and she was the only one that knew. It drove me nuts. One night we were fucking and she started it up and I started hitting her and I couldn't stop.

Show the way to self-mutilation. I like to be around you for about 24 to 48 hours and then I get sick of you. I don't like it when you tell me that you like me and want to spend more time with me. I keep my distance. On a certain level, you make me sick. Even your smell repels me. You see how I am on the third day. I don't want to know anything about your life. I like the girls that the others won't touch. The ones that get called stupid. They're not as stupid as you might think. They know me. They know I'm the Mekanik. They know why I'm around. They know I'm only good for one thing. They're careful not to get too close. I like them because they don't care. They are the truth. I use them and they use me. We don't have to play any bullshit games. It's not about that. But back to you. You're nice. A bit too nice to be hanging around with me. Do the right thing. Get the fuck away from me.

I've got my mother's intestines in a box. We all say different but for once, I'll let you women know the truth. The bottom line is that the guys just want to fuck you any way they can. I know that some of you disagree with me. I know that some of you are in love with your man and he's all you think about and you two will go skipping merrily down the lane forever and ever. You have been lied to. Let the Mekanik tell you the truth! They all want to fuck you. When you come into the restaurant with that tiny dress on, the men in the place want to stop eating their food and eat you. Sure, they love you. They love you so they can fuck you. You know when you go out with a guy, he expects you to give it up at the end of the evening like Fort Knox opening up its doors. Your idea of love is a joke to the average male. They'll say any damned thing that comes into their heads to get into your pants. Let the Mekanik tell you the truth. You've been lied to long enough! Do you ever get the feeling you're getting used? You are—every day. It's just a biomekanikal process. What the hell do you think you are? You're an animal. Your brain is nothing. Your head is spinning from love and bullshit. The words and phrases that he uses are just symbols that you have been taught to accept so you can validate your natural animal tendencies when they show themselves. You hear the right words, the right buttons get pushed and it's all you need to get it going on. You wanted to do it all the time but you needed the right way to feel about it. That's why humans are so fucked up. They must justify and feel in control of everything. You tell yourself that you're in love and presto... you're in love. But you're just in love with an idea. You're in love with a concept. Look, all they want to do is fuck you. Let the Mekanik open your eyes! There's not much to life. You feed it, clean it and make little versions of it and then die. All the things in between are acts of boredom and desperation. Civilization obviously doesn't work. You look for all this meaning in morality when the whole thing is in biology. It's so funny. Men are not much different than lab rats pushing the button to get the biscuit. They just want to fuck you. That's the way it works. I know all the best lines. That's why they call me the Mekanik. I come in and get the job done like a plumber, like a mercenary, like a Mekanik. See you in Hell, you weak sacks of shit.

Mail ordering blood and body parts. A long time ago when I loved you, I died every night thinking about you. So many sweaty nights of self-doubt, frustration and longing. When I would see you, I wanted you so badly that I hated you. I hated you because I wanted you so much. I hated you because I thought you held so much power over me. I don't think you ever knew. I was so good about covering it up. That's why I got into all those fistfights. I had to get out the frustration somehow. I used to walk by your apartment to see if your lights were on. It was half a mile out of my way home from work but I didn't care. I wanted to see if maybe you would pass by the window. I never touched you and to this day I still think about what it would have been like.

Now I'm much older and I see things differently. It's been years and I still think of you and I'll tell you why. I wish I could get as excited over a woman as I did over you. I try. I look all over for a woman who could sweep me off my feet and keep me up nights. I never find her. When I'm with a woman, I always think of you. Maybe that's how you are when you're young. In the last year it's been on my mind a lot. I long for the sleepless nights, the anger and frustration. It's the only time I feel alive. It's gone. I had it and now it's gone. I'm glad I can still remember it. It's a drag not to have that fury in my life. It was the only time I felt like I was part of something. I felt human. Now it's all nights in strange rooms clutching strangers that are as fucked up as myself. Experience screws us up. We get to a certain age and the only thing we can do is compare fresh scars to the old. All the signals become crossed and confused. I don't know what means what anymore. Back in older days, I loved and hated and could understand.

Lend me your DNA. I cannot live with one woman alone. I want all the women that I want. I want almost all the women that I see. One will not do! I love to hear them talk. Every one of them the same! Every woman is different but it all goes the same way and it all goes to the same place. It always finishes the same way. I never get tired of it! I love to make her feel that she's the only one. It's great because we both know that the other one is full of shit. They know that I, the Mekanik, has heard it all before. Every night in a different city, I love it! I love your little problems—tax, rent, trying to find a good man. I know that there's none to be found. Send in the Mekanik with the right words at the right time and it's all you need. Biology doesn't care about emotions. It all goes in the same way and ends the same way. The rest is all bullshit. It's all mekaniks. Wake up and smell the wet spot. It's the dawn of the Mekanik. It's all strings to pull and buttons to push. You thought there was more to it—like integrity, honesty. What a load! Hail the Mekanik!

The good news is that you can always move to a trailer home. You know, you should shut your fucking mouth. You blew it when you told me that you loved me. It's a good thing you were on the phone when you said that. I would have embarrassed the hell out of you in public. You talk so much shit. I would love to shove it right down your throat. Nobody loves me. You want something from me. Everybody wants something. You say you love me and then you'll use it against me later on like in some courtroom scene. Love is a weapon. It's like pulling a loaded gun on me. You should have never fucked with me. It's over. Never call me again.

24-hour abuse hotline. I thought you would be there for me. All those times you talked about having a place to go for *solace*. That's the word you used. I never heard anyone use that word before. I remember when I went to you. You stood in front of me but you weren't there. I could have reached out and touched you but you wouldn't have been there, it would have only been your flesh. Remember all the times you would come to me crying, telling me how bad it was for you and how no one wanted you and that you thought you were going crazy? I was there for you. I put everything I was doing on hold for you. Staying up for hours listening to you talk about yourself. I could have been anyone. I came to you when I needed you and found the most shallow person I have ever met.

The funny thing about it was that you didn't even notice. I was standing there bleeding at your feet and that's when you turned on the apathy full bore. I couldn't believe how much you turned to wood. It was as if you were a totally different person.

I don't trust my feelings anymore. They only seem to get me hurt. I'm scared to talk to women because I'm afraid I'll meet one that I'll like and get hurt again. I don't want to get hurt again, not like that. I never felt so stupid and alone in all my life.

Maybe I should be more like you. I shouldn't be so deep. I should live more on the surface and not let anything get to me. I'll become wooden and shallow. Vacant and apathetic, just like you, then I'll never feel this kind of pain again.

Maybe it's me that's being insensitive. Maybe you were hurt so badly that you have turned yourself off. Maybe you were once like me and really needed someone and someone used you and hurt you. Maybe you can no longer go the entire distance before you shut down. If that's the case, I wish there was something I could do. That makes me want to call you and be with you. Imagine that—two wounded people trying to help each other, two wooden people who can't even help themselves. That's how it works. Put your life under a microscope. Too sick. Pull back from the Earth's surface and look down. Just a bunch of ants running in circles. This city is so lonely.

Hey kids, take it from Sly Stallone, "Yo, if you don't go for it then someone else will." Heavy. I'm glad I caught you before you went to work. I slashed my wrists and I'm bleeding to death. No, I'm not kidding. No, it's ok. I want it like this. I wanted to tell you how much I appreciated all the help you gave me. I'm not trying to lay some kind of trip on you but I knew you would be finding out about this at some point. I wanted to talk to you so you would never have to wonder about where you and I stood with each other. No, it's ok really. I want to die. I feel good about this. I feel warm all over. It's kind of strange knowing that you're the last person that I'll ever talk to. I hope that isn't too heavy for you. BEEP! Oh, do you need to get that? No sweat. Work is work, I understand. Look, I'll hang up so I can enjoy my last few minutes alone. Good-bye my friend.

Locked in a room with Melanie Griffith. *Hi. I'm not here right now but if you'll leave your name, your number and the time you called, someone will get back to you as soon as possible.* Beep. I wish I could love you. I wish I could find something in your eyes. I wish I didn't feel so empty when I was with you. You make me feel so old. I think of you all the time. It's like a curse that has been put upon me. Do you feel it? Do you ever feel anything at all? Don't lie, look into my eyes right now and tell me how you feel. Right, you don't feel anything. I can't even get close enough to hate you. Please, at least let me hate you so I can put your memory to rest. Please don't let me keep hanging on. I'm ruining myself and you won't even return my pho... Beep.

I've got a dog named Bruce Willis. You wouldn't believe the kind of shit I've had to do to get guys to stay with me. That's why I tell you that I hate guys so much. Like this one guy I went out with. He wanted me to suck his dick all the time. If I said anything that was at all crude, he would whack me and call me a slut. What the fuck does he want? I hate guys. I don't know, maybe it's me, right? I always end up questioning myself. I had the big relationship. You know the one, the one upon which all your other relationships are based? Well the guy started fooling around with other girls right in my face. I have my pride right? So I told him to fuck off. He was in my living room crying to me about how much he loved me and this other shit. He's crying and I'm laughing in his face. I fucking hate the arrogance of men. They think that it's ok for them to fuck anyone they want but they want the women to waste their lives waiting for them. But you're different, right? You don't even think about loving me. You just want to fuck me—no hang ups, no promises. That's cool. I can deal with that. It's ok that you don't care about my life. You just want to fuck me. So, let's do it.

No, it's not rose perfume. It's fresh bullshit. The Mekanik has found a mekanikal woman. She is wonderful. She comes to me at night without all the bullshit mating ritual dinner/movie drama. We make jokes about everything. She says, "You have a cute nose." She says this every time. I tell her I'm getting a nose job. She grabs my cock and tells me that I should get a dick job while I'm there. I tell her that I'm getting it cut off next week and she laughs and says, "Then I guess you won't be calling me anymore." I ask her how's she's doing and we look at each other and break up laughing at the thought of being concerned for each other's well being. She tells me that I'm good in bed and I tell her that I'm only doing research for a book I'm working on. She says that I should take notes when we fuck. I tell her that she's giving herself too much credit because she's assuming that we are going to in the first place. She laughs in my face because she knows that I am the Mekanik. If she is there, I will fuck her if I can. I hit her with a series of questions as we undress. I ask her if she's been with any other guys. She says that she hasn't. I tell her that she better not be or I'll get jealous. We both laugh at that one. Like I give a fuck about who she's fucking. I hate those love songs where the guy is all broken up that his woman is fucking another guy. Here is this healthy young man with the world at his feet and he can't see that all he has to do is go out and get another one— maybe another five while he's at it. What a limp dick. It's hilarious to me when someone says that someone belongs to them, like, "That's *my* girl." What a crock. No one belongs to anybody. Fuck slavery, do what you want. Anyway, I seem to be straying from the point but let me say that the strong mekanikal mind wouldn't allow such mental torment over petty, trivial emotional displays such as jealousy. It's a form of laziness. You all should loosen up. The mekanikal girl that I'm talking about here has a long list of alternates. She only fucks me when she's in my area. She has options. She knows that at the end of the day it's all the same—it's all mekaniks. She gets what she wants when she wants it. She's free and she's no idiot. I only do this shit for research purposes. It's the Mekanik's opinion that you women should have more men in your life. You'll find that you will only lose if you waste your time relying on a single man for your total enjoyment. You should have a whole string of them to serve your every need. Anyway, me and the mekanikal girl go at it and have the great time we knew we would. We are mutually using each other and it's fine by us. After we're finished, she's putting her clothes back on and asks me, "Will I ever see you again?" We both break up laughing. She's funny. She gets up and leaves. That's the way it is in Mekanik Land—the land of truth.

Bend over. Here comes the art! With my poor eyesight, the woman across the room looks like you. I can make out her smile and it makes me think of you. When you smile at me, your whole face lights up. Many times that smile is accompanied by that sincere laugh you have. When you look at me, it makes me feel like I matter. Like I've done something good. When you're in a good mood and you smile at me, it feels like I'm basking in some kind of light. Actually, this is just a damn tape I play to myself. I don't find any damn warmth in your smile. The truth is that you make me feel like a creep. You don't know me, you couldn't even start to know me. Your smile is a painted-on smile. A string you learned to pull. Just thinking about it makes me cold. Looking at this woman, thinking of you, it makes me want to spit on her. Look at that smile painted on like a commercial, lying in that sucker's face. He'll be a victim of his own stupidity soon enough. Why do you treat me like that? Why do you pull me in to hurt me? Ah, fuck it. I don't need that. I don't need you. I can tell the truth from your lies. I'm still looking at that woman and thinking of you. Sure it hurts. I miss your saccharine smile. I lie to myself so well that I can't even tell when I'm telling the truth anymore. When I'm with you, I lie to myself. I tell myself that I like you. I use you to front an idea. I know you never listen to me. I tell myself that you care. It's a lie I have created for myself. My concept is nice, you should meet her sometime, ha ha ha. Oh look, she's leaving, you're leaving, you're always leaving. I won't follow her. I won't follow you. I have my idea to keep me warm—an idea of real warmth, understanding and beauty. Expansive, a wonderful lush forest of kindness. Not the crusty and brittle surface you allow me to walk endlessly and aimlessly upon. Hello, goodbye, what does it matter? You're always in the same place, right here in my mind. I'm never lonely. I'm always alone.

You've had my knife in your back long enough now! Never once have I been honest with you. All those times when you're close to me and you think you're getting closer, that's me letting you think that. I let you get a bit closer so I can get what I want. I always get what I want from you. I use the promise of love as the bait. I come on wild so you can think that you're taming me and when you think you've got me the way you want me, you give me some. All the while I'm planning the next move. It's all a game to me. It's like reeling in a fish. Give it some line, take some line, you know what I mean? It's all I can do not to laugh in your face when I see you trying to run your shit on me. What the fuck do you think I am, off the rack? You think you're playing me and all the while you're getting played like a fucking deck of cards. You think your pussy controls me? Almost everybody I know has one of those and I have been through most of them in my time and I'll be going through many more before I'm through. When I fuck, I fuck every part of you. Most men are dumber than dogshit and so easily controlled. That's where you get off, at least that's you think you get off. You're wrong. That's where I get off. I've learned to play you against yourself. I come into your life and lead you to the valley of confusion. I take you to you. It's my job. I am the Heartbreaker. I am the man who makes you hate men. I am the man who makes it hard for all the other men to ever get as close to you again. In simple words, I ruin you. I am irresistible to you and you hate both of us for it.

No way! I'm the Atomic Punk. You're Iron Man, remember? So where are they now? Your friends, I mean? You're always telling me about your friends and how you would do anything for them because they are your friends and how in return, they would die for you. I didn't believe it then and I'm not believing it now. All of your friends have gone. The good people, *your* people, that's what you would call them. It was hard to keep from laughing in your face when you talked like that. I always wondered if that's what you thought I was to you, if I was one of *your* people. You're so full of shit and now it's even too deep for you to deal with. The truth is that you don't have any friends, not now, not ever. You think you're with someone and then you find that you're just alone in a room with a stranger. You spent so much time running away from yourself, fulfilling imaginary duties to your friends that you don't even know who you are. When the shit comes down, you can't even count on yourself. Isn't that a shame. Get ready for one of the longest nights ever.

Your mother left her teeth in my shorts. Well shit, I'm not going to call her anymore. Maybe I should, just to tell her that I won't be. Fuck, I don't know. That would be the cool thing to do. At least try to be polite about the whole thing. What a mess. No. Bad idea. She'll manage to get in some kind of last word and piss me off right before she hangs up in my face and then I'll never be able to get her out of my head. I'll dwell on it until I go crazy. I know all too well what she'll say too. She'll act like she's all busy and I'll say something real heavy and she'll reply with a very breezy, "Well, whatever," like I just told her that I'm buying some shoes. And then she'll hang up right before I get to drive in the last nail of the "I don't need you anymore" insult I was going to lay on her. No, I won't call, but maybe I should. I don't hate her or anything. I just don't get along with her anymore. I know that she'll take it the wrong way and try to cover her surprise and shock with the veil of apathy. She'll end up having the last word in the relationship. No way, I won't call her. I'm just going to let it die. I know that sounds like I'm some kind of coward. Well, maybe I am but... hold on a minute, the phone... Hello?... Oh yeah, hi... I don't know, not much... Yeah I was thinking about you too... Yeah, sounds good... I'll be over in an hour. I should take a shower... Yeah ok, bye.

The Reagans had sex? They bred? Isn't there anything we can do? I'm sorry. I did a bad thing to you. I didn't realize it until now. I used you to fill a void in my life. You know I feel like such an asshole saying, "My life." Makes it sound so important. I'll explain it to you. I was never honest with you. The main reason was that I was scared. Scared of seeing too much of myself. I couldn't face you, I couldn't face myself. I couldn't face anything. I used you to shield me from myself. I used you like spackle to fill a void in me that I didn't have the guts to fill myself. I think I wasted your time and hurt your feelings. I know that it's too late now to say I'm sorry, but I thought that I would tell you. There I go again, using you to forgive myself. I think I've done this to every woman I've ever been with. Never once was it my intention to hurt anyone. I always did and I always do. That's why I keep to myself now and don't answer your calls. I'm afraid of hurting you. I'm sorry. You were the nicest person I ever spent any time with and look what I did with it.

PCP-dipped cigarettes should be called "Ozzy Osbournes". I don't like being around you. You make me deal with the truth too much. It's too intense to be with you. Why are you always like that? You take everything so goddamn seriously. Don't you ever cool out and relax? You act as if every thing were so important like life and death. I didn't want to tell you this but I will because I think it's for your own good. Everyone I know thinks you're a total asshole. I'm always having to defend you in front of other people. They always ask me what you're up to and I always tell them that you're busy and that you have too much work to do. They ask me to go out with them and would I bring you along and I have to tell them that you don't have time to go out. It makes me look bad. I can't go out and be with you. It makes me look like I don't have a life. Do you see what I mean? They think I'm a kept woman. I don't get any respect from any of my women friends. They think I'm a wimp. I tell them that they just don't understand and they laugh in my face. I'm beginning to think that maybe they're right. All you seem to have in your life is work. What am I? Chopped liver? All my friends have boyfriends and it looks like I don't. It's embarrassing to go out with them and be alone. I don't know how long I'll be able to take this. How would you like it if every time you wanted to have sex with me, I told you I was busy? You would drop me in a second. I don't know. I don't want to talk about it anymore.

He only writes that sensitive shit to get laid! Jokes lies throwaways steals lobs handoffs letdowns: I love you. You have a beautiful body. You taste good. I want to make love with you one more time before you go. I can't wait to see you again. I miss you already. Don't worry I'm not like that. No, I don't do this kind of thing all the time. I feel so good when I'm with you. It's been a long time since I've been with someone. I know that's the way it looks. I'll call you. It's always been a dream of mine to have you inside me. The last person I was with was fucked. I don't know how I fell for that same old line. He's the same as he ever was. I have a boyfriend but he won't mind—we have an understanding. I'm warning you, I have no protection. Are sure it's safe? Don't worry I pulled out way before. No it's *you* I'm concerned with, not me. Yes, I'm interested in what's on your mind—your body isn't the only thing I think about. What did you mean by that? Why are you using that tone of voice with me? I'll never forget you. You're the best. I never knew it could be like this. Luvyameanit!

You fucked my mother but I stabbed yours. She comes into the restaurant. He's been waiting all week for her only shift. This time, he's going to talk to her. He's been thinking about this all week. He's asked himself all the questions that he will ask her. He's said them all aloud a few times in the mirror so they will seem natural when he says them to her in real life. He has carried on imaginary conversations with her before he goes to sleep. He's had many different scenes. Ones where he makes her laugh, ones where he has her in tears, where she wants to take care of him and his heavy heart. When in shifts of self-pity, he has her cruel and scathing. She sends him out of the restaurant in a stoic, lonely lurch. Sometimes he comes up with the idea that they fall in love and everything is new and spectacular. He had never felt like that when he was with a woman. He had never been in love, never was knocked off his feet. He believed it could happen though. He takes walks alone through his neighborhood at night. He thinks of things she might say. Maybe it could be that she would be able to tell him things that she had never been able to tell anyone before in her whole life. He thinks of the moment that he will speak to her. It's as if his entire life has been leading up to this. So now he's in the restaurant. He's come in ten minutes before her shift so it will look like he was there and she just happened to come in. Minutes later she comes up to his table and asks if he's ordered anything other than the coffee he's drinking. He orders some food and that's it. He doesn't want to start in on her too quickly; it will seem like he's not in control of himself. Maybe he should have. No, it is better that he didn't. He's doing the right thing he tells himself. She comes by again with the food and he asks her how it is working here. She asks him what he said and he asks again but this time his voice sinks into his coffee. She looks at him and walks away. He feels a bit stupid but he's not ready to freak out. I mean, it wasn't as if he made a fool out of himself or anything. People ask other people questions all the time, right? In fact this might be just the thing he needed. She might be back there in the kitchen thinking about him right now, her curiosity working on her. Maybe she's wondering what he said, like in all those brat pack movies where the kook always gets the girl. He hears her voice right next to him. He looks up and sees her with her arms around some guy—must be her boyfriend. He sits down at a table in the corner and pours himself a cup of coffee. She sits down next to him and they start talking. At one point she says something and they both turn and look at him. He thinks fast. He just stares into his food and shovels it down. He pays and leaves. Hopefully he'll never see them on the street. He walks away as fast as he can; his stomach is turning from eating so fast. He's glad that guy came in before he made a damn fool of himself. So much for that movie garbage. Nothing like that ever happens in real life.

THE ONLY MOTHER
IS THE MOTHER OF LIES

July 01. Before I was born, I was a whore for the enlisted men. Sometimes I would be raped by more than twenty men a day. At times I was too weak to wipe their spit from my face. They would always spit on me and call me names when they were done. They told me the story of my life. "You are subhuman. What street corner were you pulled from? I want to see you in action. How much did you charge to suck dick? Maybe you paid them. I can see you on the street, crawling on your knees, pulling on men's pants as they walk home from work. They laugh down at you and run away. They can't believe what they hear coming out of your scarred mouth, 'Please, gimmie, gimmie, please.' The bums never run from you though. They like you because you do it for free. The only thing to do is annihilate you and rid the planet of your blood." They called me the "eternal whore" and said that I would never die as long as pestilence walked the earth. I tried to tell them that before I was taken to the camp, I was a computer operator and a loving husband. They laughed and handed me my wife's head. They fed me the flesh of my children. Then I was destroyed and reborn. Here I am.

July 02. I am fever running through my own veins. I infect myself constantly. I never sleep. I am alive with disease. I get better and worse. I build up resistance to myself and then I overcome myself. I live in this room. I kill roaches and call them the names of my parents. It's endless Death this time around. I remember them killing me with their fucking. I heard them through the walls. All the time fucking. I got fucked a lot in years and nightmares past. It was always rape to me. Violence, shame and humiliation is what I know. It's all I can give you.

July 03. Last night I shot a bullet into my brain. The bullet came through the other side and laughed at me. It didn't help. I thought the bullet was the magic drug—the panacea for all my ills. The only way to still my father's blood. I sat and watched the blood and brains sit on the floor. The blood cells separated into two camps: my mother's and my father's. The cells started to fight each other. It sounded like two people trying to rip each other's flesh from the bones. It smelled like ten years in an isolation cell. I was born with too much blood and brains. All of my mother's and father's blood and brains. They shoved all their brain cells into my head and sometimes the pressure is so much that all I can do is scream.

July 04. Listen to the bullet night. Hear them fly by. I call them insects. It's the most common sound in my part of the Death Star. Another day passes. The hallways and streets smell like Death, always Death. The smell of brains and blood fills my mind. Humans are screaming horror trips. Flesh covered pain dealers. Pain is what I was born with. I have no talent except the ability to take pain—lifetimes of pain. It's all Death to me. You can't take my eyes away from it. I was strapped down and tied to the sounds of fucking. I was raised by the molesting hands of strangers. I cannot stand to be touched unless it's done violently. If I'm going to fuck, then it's rape and I want to have the bruises. It's no good unless I feel like ripping my guts out and vomiting years of screaming into pillows.

July 05. Hi, I'd like you to meet my girlfriend, the junkie. Isn't she swell? No, I don't hit her, she gets those bruises all by herself. Tell the nice man how you put that needle in yourself all the goddamn time like some fucking lab animal. Go on, tell the man the things he wants to know. He might be good to you. He might give you a taste and that's all you live for, right? You'd like a little taste wouldn't you? Wouldn't you? Yeah it looks like she has bite marks all up and down her arms. She thinks she's so fucking smart. She talks a lot of shit to me when she's high, you know? She puts me down and laughs at me, but when she needs that taste she'll say anything to get what she needs. I think it's her mother and father who drove her to it. I know I sure as hell didn't. She was fucked up and used when I got to her. You know how the parents will fuck up their offspring. That's why I hate mine. They'll try to kill you. They are so busy with their fucked up plane-about-to-crash lives that all they can bring to the kid is pain. You know, I don't know how any of us make it as far as we do. Look at her. What a dried up piece of shit she is. I keep her around to remind me of all the things that I don't want to turn into.

July 06. Holy killer man. Walking down the street with a Dooms-day in his hand. Hot light chain gang man. Hot night dog breath man. Walking down the street with a flower in his hand. Big time all mine man. You bet your dead ass man. Cleaning up the streets with a sickle in his hand. I've got your eyes in my fist. You see what I want you to see. I want you to see it all. I've got your life all planned. You'll be what I want you to be. I want to see you crawl. I've got something for you. You're going to get it. Over and over.

July 07. Hateful shit. It's all around. If you take half a second to look, you'll see it. It's all you'll see. He hit her in broad daylight at an intersection. I was waiting at the bus stop and saw the whole thing. I didn't do anything because I didn't want to get involved. On the way there, I stepped in some dog shit. It would be something if the dog belonged to that couple. It would be good to go to their house and shoot the dog right on their front porch. I say out loud the things that you think. You can call me all the names you want but you know that you feel the same way. You're always quick to judge. You're good at making little names for people. You give them little roles. You put them in little boxes but you don't put yourself in one. You're an individual. They're all assholes, right? Like the way you are in traffic. Yelling at all of them, wishing they would all go die. If I had a dime for every time I wanted to kill someone, I know how rich I'd be. You're no different. You know when you're out somewhere and you hear two people talking in a language that you can't understand, you think that maybe they are telling each other mysterious fascinating things? Bullshit. They're talking about getting laid and how poor they are and how fucked everything is.

July 08. I'm in the hot room again. I am a time junkie. I am a user. I have come to the point to where I ask myself who's using whom. I take a look around, I see what I do to time. I look in the mirror and I see what it's doing back to me. I have come to the conclusion that we got a pretty good thing going. I abuse time. I starve it. I bore it to madness. Some nights I sit still for hours trying to make time go insane. I have devoted my life to making time pay. I want to see it bleed. I want to be the king of scars and then I want to throw it away.

July 09. I'm sitting in a four-walled hot room. 3:40 a.m. I am alone and clammy skinned. I think of her hot body. I close my eyes and kiss her beautiful mouth. I wrap my lips around her nipple. She pulls my head into her breast. I suck and lick and kiss. Our bodies start to sweat; her ribcage grinds against mine. We are rolling in a field of fire, our bodies cut and bleeding. We have no names—we are blissfully insane... I open my eyes and I see the walls again. Sweat is running down my face and back. My teeth are tightly clenched. Now I want to kill. I want to be a war machine. I close my eyes and see a man with a flamethrower torching a school yard of kids. I see the bodies scattered across the smoking blacktop. The smell is acrid and heavy... I open my eyes and I feel like the last man on earth. I feel so empty that I think I'm going to cave in. If only she would come and touch me, talk to me... anything. I can smell her hair. I can taste her neck. I replay the times at her house in my mind like movies. As I do this I realize I'm making it much better than it actually was. I look around the room—I'm still alone. I wait for sleep. It's temporary death for me. In sleep I can run away from myself and not even the dreams can reach me. This is the only time I am free. Every waking moment I am chained to my mutilated, sweating, greasy body. I can't take my eyes from the wall for long periods of time. I try to move but I can't seem to do it. My body forces me to stare at the wall; it drives me into myself. Every waking moment I pound myself like a nail into my skull.

July 10. Locked in an insane dream. It's like a television I can't turn off. Sometimes I want to rip my face off and get out. Hack open a hole in my ribcage and get the fuck out. I stand in front of the mirror and stare at my face. Sometimes I think that something is going to rip out of my forehead. I will suddenly be overcome with an overpowering feeling of claustrophobia. It took me awhile to understand but now I know. I am locked in solitary. Sometimes I feel like my face is pressed up against the roof of my skull. My head becomes a bad place to be. I used to think that there was someone else in there with me. I couldn't believe I would do all this to myself. But now I know that it's all me and it's all up here. I sometimes wish to get driven out of my mind. That would be so good. Like a vacation, but I don't think it's going to happen. I accept what I am becoming. I am unable to stop it. This is what I want.

July 11. I hear a pig's radio outside. I look out the window. There is a youth getting talked to by a pig. The only part of the conversation I can hear is the pig's. The boy is talking too low. "Where did you get that bike? You know we get about fifty arrests a month out of that apartment building. Fifty arrests. Felonies, people go to prison. Where did you get that bike? Okay, we have two warrants out for your arrest. Put your hands behind your head..." I hear the click of the handcuffs. The boy is put in the car. The bike is put in the trunk. The car drives off.

July 12. I fell down. Down through the smiling pictures. Down through the brightly lit hallways. A fall down dance with shit on my shoes. I'm falling through your face. Skull bone framework is such a dirty house. Can't get clean. Falling dirty. Falling mean. Cut glass eyes. Weeping urine dog man. Falling on my knees. Falling down. Cutting my hand on savage alley floors. Using the word *pathetic*. Feeling the knife. Feeling a stranger's shoes between my ribs. Piss falling like rain on my head. Falling like rain. Burning rain. Falling down. End.

July 13. I want to make you feel it like you made me feel it. I want to make you taste the fear and the pain that you made me taste. I want you to know me. I want you to live my pain. I want to give it to you like you gave it to me. It's the least I can do. I want to fill your guts with hate. I will make you hate them. I will make you hate yourself. I will enter you like a disease, like a curse. I will inject you with the nightmares that you gave me. I will give you a gun without bullets. I will make you live it to the end. I'm going to fill you with electric shock. I'm going to drill you hollow with the emptiness you filled me with. I'm going to take back all the things that you took away from me and give you back all the things that you gave me. I will make you wish you never were. I promise.

July 14. Please save me. I can't do it myself. Come down into my hole and shoot me in the head. I don't have the guts to do it myself. You will be the bullet of my dreams. I want you to shoot me. It's what I want. Yours will be the sweating hand that gets me out of the mess that I cannot. You will be the hero in the heaving dream. You are my only hope. When the bullet rips through my brain, all the filth and shame and guilt will fall away. The great weight will fall off my shoulders. I can't live with all these people on the planet. I understand that it's me with the problem. I can't afford to kill them all so I want you to kill me. Exterminate me. I am the one of a kind who cannot take it, who will not take it. I am outnumbered, millions to me. There's no way out except all the way out. I want to suck the bullets from your gun. I want to leech all the Death that I can from you and then that might not even be enough. Do it like a lover. Make my life mean something by taking it all the way away. You have no idea what joy you will bring me. The bullet. Yes, the bullet. I am too strong to live. My will forces me to be destroyed for the better of my one of a kind. Human nature is fighting me. Keeping me from doing what needs to be done. Come down into my hole and shoot me in the head.

July 15. I wish I was made of cardboard so I could rip parts of myself off and not have to see them anymore. I wish it wasn't illegal to hurt myself to make myself feel better about having your blood in my body. I remember the one guy who was waiting for you to come out to the living room one night. He told me you suck dick real good—the best he ever had. That's all I need to hear. You put me through a living hell, you and that cunt of yours. Never could get enough of that dick, could you? The other guy who used to feel me up, he was a real winner. He used to rub my pussy through my dress. I should shoot you. I should burn your skin with hot knives. I should stab you over and over until your blood covers the floor. Your other boyfriend who used to get his kicks by beating the shit out of me with a belt. Tell me where he lives. I want to have a talk with him. I was small then and I couldn't do anything about it and now I'm crazy and full of pain and I want to mutilate him. Don't hide him from me. He's mine.

July 16. I've got a double brain, two times insane. They cut you down and they throw you away. You no longer have what they want. They throw you away and you see how everything gets this sameness about it when it begins to rot. They'll pull you down a long road and tell you that snakes are filthy creatures who live in the dirt. I live in the dirt. Do you know what I see when I open my eyes? I see what I am looking at. I know that you want to destroy me. You want to choke my soul. Of course that will never happen. I am the eternal whore. The secret hero. Undeniable. Unbreakable. Beyond pain and suffering. Divine.

July 17. From now on, all you get is my wrath. From now on, all you see is your reflection mirrored in my fist. All bets are off. The one trick pony is kicking the thoroughbreds and it never felt better. From the fortress, I sniper-fire. From the left side of my brain, I stab and mutilate. From a privileged position, I drop fire. Want to evolve? Learn to duck. Don't be afraid to get your clothes dirty diving for cover because things are different now. The gloves are off, you weaklings. So many years I carried you. So many years I served you. So much time I spent trying to do the right thing for you. It was all for nothing. I'd like to put all of you in concentration camps so you could concentrate. Kill you and then kill the killers. You're no better than what you think you're superior to. You were wrong and you'll always be wrong. The human shield has stepped to the side and now it's all going to hit you. I will erase you. The final insult will be seeing how easy you fold.

July 18. Small room with a window the size of a postcard. Every day a different postcard is inserted depending on what they want to do to the patient. Lights on and off. Pictures of wife and family being mutilated are occasionally slipped into the window. Sounds are constantly coming in through the speakers in the cell. It's all controlled of course. The patient is occasionally fed the soundtrack of a pornographic movie while the sounds of sirens and car crashes fade in and out constantly. Sound is used as punishment for those who resist treatment.

The facility is for those having problems fitting into society. There is a waiting list years long to get in.

The walls are grey. The lights are fluorescent. The patient's clothes are grey. There are no mirrors. Some patients have been known to grow their nails out and claw themselves to produce blood, just to see some color.

"After 7 1/2 months in the grey room, I lost all concept of color. My dreams, my thoughts were devoid of color. I nearly lost my mind in there. I'm better now. I've learned how to use it to my advantage."

Patients have been known to defecate on the floor next to the small hole in the floor for waste and stare at their own excrement just to have something to give them contrast.

"There came a point where I would close my eyes and instead of being black, it was grey. I could not escape the grey. Every thought turned against me. I could swear that I would try to kill myself in my dreams. You know those dreams like when you're falling off a cliff or something and you wake up right before you hit the ground? I started having dreams like that every night, except I would not wake up when my body would hit the ground. I would land on concrete and just get up. I had one dream where I had thrown myself off of an apartment building about three or four times. I got up and started crying. I'll never forget it. I started begging God to let my body shatter on the ground. I got up to throw myself off again. I jumped and when I landed that time, there was a trampoline waiting for me. I started trying to choke myself to death but somehow I would always wake up."

Doctors reason that the elimination of all color gives the patient the effect that closely resembles a lobotomy.

"We defuse the patient's color scheme. We strip him down emotionally, spiritually and mentally. Then of course, we rebuild the patient with what we consider good, moral and socially acceptable traits. And of course, since there is no cutting or burning of any of the frontal lobes, there is no permanent or lasting ill effects from this treatment... at least none that we can see at this time."

I can't see you. The light is in my eyes.

July 19. Walking down their streets, rubbing elbows with them. Don't you sometimes want to lean over and take a bite and watch the colors come out? I do. Sometimes I go out there and they scare me, they freak me out. Makes me think they all know something that I don't, that they're just waiting for me to follow along and get into line. They watch me and quietly wait. They freak me out. Murderers, killers, monsters with suits on, smiling at me like how a doctor smiles, like how an airplane pilot smiles. Sometimes I scare myself when I think how I once believed them. I got myself a one man tribe and I am secretive as shit because I know what happens when you see a lake of placid water or a beautiful bird. You kill it. You make it yours.

July 20. I will fill your dreams with black snakes. My hands crushing your throat. Fists through scar tissue. Years of walking through blasted parking lots while you sucked ten miles of cock. I will take you straight to hell. You will know endless pain. I will destroy your life. This is it. I am where all things end up. I am the definition of your Death. I live to terminate you. After I burn your body, I will go to the grave of your mother and kill again. I will kill you and kill you. I am a machine. Monster. I have no mind. No life. I am a machine covered with scar tissue and I am coming to end your dreams. Break your bones. Turn you into ash. You useless swine.

July 21. The telephone poles in my neighborhood look like large crucifixes. I was looking at them as I was walking down the street tonight. I'd like to nail a pig to every one of them. You're driving in your car and you see a man nailed to a light pole, naked except for a pair of jockey shorts. His gut hangs over his waistband. You can see the large bruises where he has been beaten. You keep driving and you keep seeing pigs' bodies nailed to telephone poles. The bodies show various forms of mutilation: burn marks, eyes removed, penises and testicles hacked off and shoved into their mouths. Miles of dead pigs rotting in the sun all the way to the beach. Strange fruit indeed! Beautiful girls in cars driving to the beach to get tanned will see them. Everyone will see them. These pieces of shit blew it while they were here. Pigs suck. Fuck 'em.

July 22. Every time I come I have a fixed image in my head— usually some porno shot that I've seen recently. It's hardly ever about the girl that I am with at the time. The other night I was fucking and I was right about to come and this time I tried something different. I flashed to a picture of a pile of dead bodies in Belsen. Here I was with this girl who's wrapped around me and all I can think about is a bunch of stiffs. Didn't make a shit bit of difference though. It felt the same as any other fuck I ever had in my life.

July 23. I saw on a television show that people who commit suicide often had fucked up childhoods. Those who were abused by their parents blame themselves. The stress shows up in later life, late 20's early 30's. Celebrities come out with books detailing the abuses suffered at the hands of their parents and stepparents. People shoot themselves in the head after raping their sons and daughters and it's found out that the same was done to them. The way they get back at the parents is to take their own life. On the way, they manage to take a few with them. It's as if some invisible hand comes up and grabs my throat when I try to speak about my father. He controls me still. I want to kill myself all the time. I cannot accept love on any level. I have tried and I see through it time after time. I have tried to love women and it never works. After a few days, I feel sick. Whenever someone tells me they love me, I think of my mother and blood.

July 24. It's hot outside now that the sun swings earlier and later. The heat is everywhere. It's 360 degrees outside! The noise and the colors are alive and crawling up and down your wall, and it's hot, and you can feel it. You feel like you're water in a boiling kettle. Oh son, I can see you plain as day. You're going into that filthy bathroom to beat your brains into the sink. Are you going to beat it off or are you gonna rip it off and throw it across the room? Madness, like the condensation running rabid seeing-eye dog through your brain. And by the way, how is that brain of yours? That sick motherfucking puking desperate weak animal? Is it hot yet? Is it cooking yet? It's 360 degrees outside. Inside, is it burned to a crisp yet? Well? Look at that stupid grinning, drooling shrink-wrapped face looking back at you. It's 360 degrees outside, inside, everywhere. You're surrounded. Come out with your hopes up. 360 degree heat will cut you down. 360 degree heat will chop your praying hands right off. They'll slip right down the drain real slow. You leave a little of yourself everywhere you go as life slips away.

July 25. All I gotta do is touch the glass belly of my war dream and I'm Superman again. I see you walking down the streets of this city. You're all insects and reptiles. Your existence revolves around me. There is a swastika on the rising sun. I'm going to get on that train and ride into my head through the back. Smash through my skull. Shiny molten tracks. Greasy steel train, jaw clenched slamming down the line. My reflection in the mirror, florescent lights, eyes dead crawling into the backs of the sockets. Cheeks fallen in. I look insolent, sullen and stupid.

July 26. God doesn't ride on subways. I'll be waiting for you down there. Walk to the bottom of the stairs. Man-made cement asshole. Fuck this small talk. Violence is the only thing you understand besides money and fear. I'll be there when you come to ride. You'll scream when I grab your collarbone. Ride through the darkness all night long.

July 27. When I look out the window and see the trash piling up, when I see those jokers out there walking with their mates, I want to be Superman. I want to walk up to one of them and say the right shit that will push one of their stupid buttons and they'll try to get me to fight and I'll laugh and blow the piece of shit's face off. I can blow them up anytime I want. It would feel good to be a good god for once. If there was a god, he fucked up. He let them get away with too much. There should be more natural disasters. I like those because you can't blame anyone. You can't put an earthquake on trial. You can't send a flood to the chair. Look at the fucking zoo that I live in. All these bent up little players running around through the ruins saying, "Isn't it groovy and decadent? Cool!" Looking like Death and thinking they're something. I would like to help. I really would. I wonder if the guy at the gun store would give me a discount on the bullets I'll need if I told him what I was up to.

July 28. I see myself as some kind of superhero. I like to close my eyes and imagine myself with a machine gun running through the neighborhood killing all the kids on the block because they remind me of the ones who used to chase and hit me. I used to have to hide from them when I should have been out dragging them into garages and stabbing them and leaving them for their parents to mourn over. If I can kill all these little fuckers before they grow up to be big fuckers, then I will be saving the world. I think more children should be aborted. Families with more than one child should have to choose the one they like the best and then the others will be taken away and incinerated. Look at the streets full of these idiots running wild with no clue. They pollute and kill. I don't mind the killing but they don't kill each other fast enough for my liking. They deal drugs all night long underneath my window. Not the right kind of drugs either. It would be better if it was pure poison so they would get real high once and then die and leave me alone. All highs should be lethal injections. Kill and keep killing. Freedom is too big an idea for these weak pieces of shit. I want to be God, the almighty superhero. I want to see it all burn down to the ground.

July 29. The doctors are running out of patients. I ran out of patience a long time ago. Now I just run. I run along the winding river bed. Running for my life? Running from my life? Are you one in a million or are you the one in a million? I hope that the waves of courage don't steal my fear away.

July 30. The thing that keeps me from killing more of you is that I know that you don't know what you're fucking with. You think that nothing will ever happen to you. So many times you have passed me in the street never knowing that I found three ways to kill you before you were even within spitting distance of me. When you talk shit, I can tell that you're used to getting away with it. I love the look of surprise on your face when I have broken it with my fist. To be raised with violence dealt by intellectuals is a privilege. Most people get one and not the other. The combination is deadly. To realize your mortality and the fragile mortality of anything that breathes without a morally judgmental view gives you an insight that raises you above the normal consciousness. It's a hard road to walk. You're not up to it, believe me. I always hear you use terms and words that you have no right to use. "No reason" is one. You're saddened when someone is killed for what you think is no reason. There's a reason for everything that happens. You just can't see most of them. That's why there is so much mystery and confusion in your life. That's why you believe in fate and luck. "Senseless" is a word you like to use to describe the actions of others but never your own. You have no idea how fucking senseless you are and you never will. "Nothing" is another word you throw around. You have no idea what nothing is. Your life is too full of shit to ever get to something as huge as nothingness.

July 31. I'm going to trade places with the sun. I will be unrelenting fire and the sun will be an animal bag of water looking not to get killed by the weaklings of civilization. I will hang high in the sky and look down upon the earth. I will inch closer and closer as the days pass. In a short period of time, I will be burning the planet to the ground. It's the only thing I want to do. I want to be the first and only real god there ever was. No god would have let it go this far without destroying the place. Natural disasters are just not frequent enough. I can close my eyes and imagine all the forests and cities burning. Fuck the rain forests. Fuck the ghettos. Fuck the pigs. No more prisons. No more lies. No more pain. No more history books full of misinformation. None of it will matter. There will be no more history besides the things that I know. The planet will be perfect—a black planet. Black is the color of peace. Black is the color of armies burnt to a crisp. There will be no more pollution. The earth will be able to start all over again. I will stand alone and silent waiting to burn it to the ground again. Me, the eternal whore. The mother of all lies.

SUFFOCATION
AND
SOLITUDE

You can understand the couple in the apartment next to yours. The man—shirt wet with sweat, veins in his neck bulging like they're going to burst. Eyes about to shoot out of his head and splatter against the wall. He's screaming at his wife, "You fucking bitch, she's fucking a nigger! You've known about it for months and you didn't tell me! I should kill you bitch! You're probably fucking one too! A spade, a fucking nigger monkey spade!" He's sweating profusely now. She cringes against the refrigerator. She winces at every word. His mouth is flecked with spit and tobacco. He grabs her by the armpits and slams her repeatedly against the refrigerator. Her head hits the freezer door handle and she starts to bleed. Blood pours down the back of her neck onto her print dress. The blood mixes with the sweat and the edges of the stain are pink. The stain on her dress starts acting like a small printing press as he slams her, printing small blood blotches against the paint. Blood is matting her hair against her neck. Her legs give out. She slides to the floor leaving a long greasy trail. She has known. She met the boy and even though she was scared at first, she has come to like him. She can see what her daughter sees in him. He's polite, more polite than any of the other men she's brought by. He picks her up and backhands her. The world goes crooked and she feels something hit her hard on the side. It's her body hitting the floor. She blacks out.

I am a man fired out of the barrel of a gun
I see explosions rising from the street
I am hot and walking forever through this mess
The heat is searing
Every moment I am being cooked alive
The sidewalk does not end
There is no end to the insanity

I cross an intersection
I see a man handcuffed to a light pole
Men, women and children are beating him with sticks
I keep walking
I'm starting to melt
I see a man on a leash, he's crawling
His wife is kicking him
He's barking and yelping like a dog
Up ahead a man pulls out a gun
Fires six shots into his head
He throws down the gun in disgust and walks away
I see a priest with a flamethrower
He hoses down a group of bums sitting on a porch
People are hanging out of their windows cheering
I step over a pile of severed cocks
I see a line of people
A man at the front gives another man some money
The man takes the money and shoots him in the head
Men are fighting each other to get ahead in the line
The ground starts to shake
I know that salvation is on the way
Until that day comes
Freedom is such a poor excuse

She was the first one of her friends to get an abortion. By the time they graduated high school, she had gotten one more and four of the other girls had gotten one as well. Out of the six total, only one of the boys had helped out in any way whatsoever. All the other guys said either it was not them or fuck off. Every time one of the girls got "preggers", the other ones swore off sex completely. This lasted about a month at the very best. Those nasty boys didn't give a fuck. They didn't. They were always ready to shove their thing right into you but when it came time to pay the consequences, they acted like they didn't even know who you were.

She got her third abortion the summer after graduation. All summer long she played that "pull it out right before you come" thing that never works but makes sense it you're horny and stupid. She was a lot of both. It was a beautiful summer, not too hot, just right for hanging around and having a good time.

To make a long story about pimply, overweight, pasty white-skinned teenagers having noisy sex in the back of third-hand cars in parking lots, alleys and other likely places, short and to the point—the third one killed her. She died in the middle of a convulsive fit. Septic infection, goddamn thing was done in Beverly Fucking Hills too. The boy even paid for half of it.

None of her friends came to the funeral a week later. They were too busy popping birth control pills and cramming big lifeguard's cocks into every conceivable orifice in the air conditioned luxury of Malibu condominiums.

A car hits a boy riding a motorcycle at the intersection of Artesia and Phelan Ave. The front tire of the car locks on the boy's head and drags it across the intersection. The red streak turns brown and stays there all summer.

July 4, 1971, Washington DC. Downtown is packed with people from all over to see the fireworks. White tourists lay down blankets on the lawn. They sit and eat the lunches they brought. Groups of black youths rove through them asking if they can have some food, asking if they can use their frisbees or footballs, then taking them and laughing in their cracker faces knowing that the father won't get up to get the item back.

The circular sidewalk that surrounds the monument is packed with people taking pictures and checking out the other national monuments. Weaving through them are black youths on ten-speed bikes blowing whistles and shouting obscenities as they go. A white boy with a bike stands and watches them as they ride around the circle. A black boy approaches him, grabs the handle-bar of the bike and asks him if he can try the bike out. The boy frowns slightly scared, wondering if he'll get his bike back or get beaten up. He gives the bike to the boy who gets on it and rides it over to his other friends. He points to the boy and they all start laughing. The boy rides the bike down one of the walkways and onto the street and disappears with his shirt tails flapping in the wind.

Three black youths walk up to a young white couple that are carrying a basket between them. The smallest of the three goes up and pulls the handle of the basket. The girl drops her side immediately. The guy doesn't give in and pulls on the basket and says, "Hey man, please, be cool." The boy drops the basket handle and walks backwards. One of the other boys walks up and punches the man in the mouth. The man drops the basket and backs off holding his face. Without a word, the smallest boy takes the basket. The boys walk away. The couple walk back to their car and go back to wherever the fuck they came from.

A Marine gets in a scuffle with a man he sees taking a basket from a woman. The Marine is beating the man. The man is backing away yelling obscenities. The police come and both are arrested and put in the back of the same car and taken away.

The mayor is supposed to give a speech right before the fireworks are set to go off. No one cares. They all want to see the fireworks and get the hell out of downtown.

The man and the Marine both spend the weekend in jail. A seventeen year-old boy is stabbed in the thigh when he resists some other boys who try to take his bike. People watch the entire episode and do nothing. A fistfight erupts in a parking lot between two men over a parking space. One punches the other in the side of the head, killing him instantly. The man calls the police himself and waits to be arrested. A man walks into a parking garage to get his car. He comes upon another man trying to break into it. He beats the thief until he is on the ground passed out. He kicks the unmoving body a few times and drags it between two cars and gets in his car and drives off. He goes to the local bar and tells his friends about the whole thing. He takes them out into the parking lot and shows them where the guy tried to break in. "See look at where the spook chipped the paint." His friends buy him drinks and watch the news about all the shit happening downtown on television and laugh at the reports of the crime and say to each other that it serves them right. You go there and mix with those animals, you deserve what you get.

The sun is setting, the fireworks are going to go off soon. Undercover cops bust an eighteen year-old girl with over one hundred joints. She is cuffed and led away. Two small children shoot at each other with cap guns. When they shoot at each other, they both fall down in mock death and get up laughing hysterically. They do this until all the caps run out. A young boy vomits the contents of his stomach onto his mother's lap: a white bread and bologna sandwich, a pint of milk and a large quantity of caramel popcorn.

I ran through the jungle
I swung from heat trees
I watched everything around me burn and disintegrate
I walked through the desert
I swam up a river of sweat
I had glorious hallucinations
Visions of the iron soul
Ten mating seasons
Crammed into one day of explosive, convulsive activity
Large piles of bodies burning in the desert
Men driven insane, screaming at the sun
Spitting out chunks of their tongues
I crawled on the cinder trail
I talked to the old man in the hole
I walked to the dark places
I walked down the stairs
I felt the cool air on my face
I surfaced in the darkness
I walked through a slum
Looked like a war had been there before me
The street lights made everything look naked and bloodshot
There were dead bodies in the trees
I felt like a soldier on a long march
I ran through a hot rainstorm
I wanted to break down
I wanted to cave in and turn to dust
Self-destruction was the star that hung burning above me
I wanted to rip myself limb from limb
I thought if I kept walking long enough through the night
I would pass myself
I would see myself as a stranger

I would attack
I would mutilate
I would destroy
Myself
Annihilation of self
The perfect self-contained struggle
I fell short of totally nullifying myself
Morbid fascination kept me hanging on
Too much self-hatred to die
I saw the trees vibrate
I waited for busses to explode
I walked by her house
I looked into her window
I saw her corpse behind the pane
Beyond the pain
I saw myself standing next to her
My body was gutted, my eyes were ripped out
There was a sign around my neck
Love kills
From the east I heard an alarm sound
The sun was coming
Soon they would be all over the place
Crawling like ants
Slobbering and panting
I found a place to hide and wait

War soundtrack. I need to hear war sounds while I fuck. Otherwise I feel dead. I can't come. I need to feel good. If I'm impotent tonight, I will beat you. War is here. I can find no love in the eyes of peace. Please give me war. I want to love you. I want to kill you. I want to hate you. Let me hate you. Let me love you. Let me in.

Let me stab you. I want to love you. I want to kick you. For the rest of my life over and over. In the eyes of love, there is no love. War now so I can have you. You are what I want. After we come, let's go out. We'll kill some of them. We will rape their weakness, plunder their fear. We will destroy them. We will incinerate them. It's only them. Annihilate them. We will love them to death. We will violate them completely. We will turn them to ash with our love. Our love will be the salvation. Our love will be the answer.

He went into the bathroom of the theater to take a leak. His girlfriend was in her seat. He had his back to the door, cock out, pissing into the urinal. The man grabbed his head and slammed it into the tile wall. Before he could reach up or turn around to see his attacker, the man slammed his head into the flusher. He felt his teeth give way with a brittle crunch that thundered in his ears. That's all he remembered. The next thing he knew, he was in the lobby of the city hospital emergency room, sitting in a wheelchair with his girlfriend sitting across from him. His wallet was gone. His face felt like it was going to fall off. The cab came and took them to their respective homes.

Selective memory 3X. He only sucked and got sucked. The other thing was much too violent and gross for him to even think about. One night he got worked over in an alley behind a local bar. He was on the ground and they were kicking him while screaming, "You goddamnmotherfuckingfaggotqueer!" Each syllable was accented with a hard kick to the ribs or head. The guys doing it thought it was a lot of fun, *whatthefuck, it's only a faggot,* and went back into the bar laughing and making faggot jokes.

They never saw the faggot again. In fact by the next round, they had forgotten about the guy.

He got her pregnant and he left her. She didn't know what to do. She was too scared to get an abortion. She was too scared to have the kid and be its mother. She jumped off the roof of her apartment building. When he found out, he was troubled. His troubled feelings soon gave way to relief. In a few weeks he had forgotten about it. Soon he was just another swingin' dick walking down the street.

She told the police on her boyfriend. They nailed him with a suitcase full of speed. He was tried and sent to jail. She was paid in full the money that she was promised for helping out. She moved into a nice apartment. After a while, she got some letters from him. He didn't know she set him up. His letters were full of declarations of eternal love, and how the only thing that kept him going was thinking of her each and every day as he sat in his rotten, stinking cell. She laughed at the letters and threw them away. After a few months, she stopped reading them. She would get them and treat them like someone treats junk mail. After about nine months, the letters stopped. She didn't notice.

The neighborhood got together and helped watch each other's houses to try to cut down on the crime rate. Every night, one of the residents would make a sweep of the neighborhood with their car. Signs were put up in the windows of every house saying that there was a neighborhood watch in effect. The effort worked; the crime rate went down drastically.

One night, one of the residents actually made a citizen's arrest. He caught a burglar trying to break into his next door neighbor's kitchen window. Later that month, there was a block party. All of the neighbors were there. They had all pitched together and sprung the guy out of jail. He was brought to the picnic in a squad car. He was tied to a pole and beaten to death. His body was dragged into the street and doused with gasoline and torched. Everyone clapped and cheered as the flames made the body crackle and sizzle.

When I was five, Tom's father had a birthday party for him in his backyard. He invited me and all of my friends from school. We showed up on Saturday as planned. Tom's dad was running around getting things ready, cooking hot dogs and hamburgers and making kool aid by the pitcher. He insisted that all the kids call him by his first name, George. Everything was going real great. I bet Tom felt real important, watching his dad doing all this stuff for him and his friends. We all started playing some game, I don't remember what it was. After a while, I noticed that Tom's dad and my friend Frank were not around. I heard screams from inside the house. The back porch door flew open and Frank came running out screaming and crying. Tom's dad came out right behind him. Frank turned and screamed for his mother and father over and over. He pointed at Tom's dad and said, "I'm telling, I'm telling!" He ran out the back gate and down the block. We all just kind of stood there looking at each other. Then we all turned and looked at him. About ten minutes later, Frank's dad came into the backyard with a baseball bat. He screamed, "Where is the sonofabitch? I'm gonna kill him!" We were all still standing there. One of the kids pointed at the house and said that he was in there. We all watched Frank's dad beat up Tom's dad with the bat. Tom's dad was on the front lawn with his hands over his head as Frank's dad beat him. The cops came and pulled Frank's dad off of him. An ambulance came and took Tom's dad away. As the ambulance was leaving, my mother pulled up in her car and told me to get in and wait. She got out and talked to the cops for a long time and we drove back to her apartment. Tom's family moved.

She called it rape. He called it *enforced love*. She said that it was a vile intrusion. He said that it was *doing what came naturally*. She called it marriage. He called it *minimum security prison*. They started talking about Heaven and Hell. I got up and left the room.

Hanged himself two weeks later. They took him underneath the stairs. He said, "Please let me go. Don't make me do this. Please-god-man-fuck." One of them hit him in the mouth. He sucked all their cocks with tears in his eyes. After he was done, they took his money and split. He got up and vomited until he thought he was going to choke himself to death and then he climbed up the steps and somehow got home.

I walked into a 7-11 in Virginia. Some Marines were giving the two Indian cashiers a hard time. It was after midnight and the store was not allowed to sell them beer. They told the cashiers that the one down the road let them do it all the time. The cashier was telling him that it wasn't he who made the rules up. Then one Marine said to the others, "Well, I guess we should just go over the counter and beat the shit out of these two assholes." At that moment, the Marines and the cashiers turned and looked at me. I just stood there and waited to see what was going to happen. One of the cashiers started laughing this real twisted laugh, and said, "Beat us... right. Ha ha ha." And he kept on laughing and his eyes started to bug out of his head. The Marines started to look at each other. I saw the cashier make a move and I backed off down an aisle. He came out with a baseball bat and stood to their left side. He started banging the bat on the ground saying, "Beat me. Beat me my friend. Yes, yes. Ha ha."

Summer isolation insanity machine. Napalm in the womb. Blood-shot eyes crawl the streets, looking for something that's not dead. Watch me terminate this command. Watch me incinerate this impotent dream. Watch me annihilate this vision. Walking straight lines up the alley of their assholes. Dark, dark and getting darker. It's time to destroy the lie. Watch me slash and mutilate their womb. Whip it 'til it's thick. Melt the streets. Stack them up and burn them. Let them burn the sun to cinder.

A woman pours gasoline over herself and her infant child. She lights a match and the two of them go up in flames.

A man ate his own head. Broke it open with a hammer. Ate the white and the grey. Cut his nose, ears and lips off. Ate them too. Punched his teeth down his throat. Swallowed his eyes. Ran out of things to eat, didn't have the brains to care.

A man sells little crosses with roaches nailed to them.

A beautiful woman does a striptease on a lit stage. The men in the crowd applaud and yell. She is beautiful and she's letting it all show. She grinds and pushes it out to the guys. They're losing their minds. She keeps it going, really makes it hot. She bends down and shakes it. She picks up something wrapped in a handkerchief. She pulls the handkerchief off—it's a gun. She turns to the men and starts sucking and tonguing the barrel. She really gets into it and so do the guys. Her head moves faster and faster. She plants her feet and pulls the trigger, blowing her brains all over the room.

They were in love. Fucking and fighting all the time. They lived in a small apartment. It smelled of insecticide and dirty clothes. It was so hot at night that neither of them could sleep, so they either fought or fucked. It all sounded the same to the neighbors—shit flying through the air and smashing against the wall, screaming and cussing and bedboard banging against the wall. One August evening, two women were walking down the hall to their apartment. They walked by the couple's door and stood a moment to listen. The normal combat soundtrack was going down. One said, "I thought they loved each other. It sounds like they are trying to kill one another to me." The other said, "I think that love is finding your favorite person to hate, and giving it all you've got." The other nodded and they walked on.

He's drunk again
He comes storming into the house like a confused emperor
He sees me and says
"There you are, you creep."
He starts to kick me lightly in my side
His parents wouldn't appreciate it if I dropped him right there in the living room
Liquor and Tobacco clings to him as he walks past
That smell
Smells like Losers
Smells like hate
Smells like nowhere
Makes me wonder if the guy in the Marlboro ad ever smells like that. If he walks off the set hacking and spitting out bitter brown

snot, cursing the good life. Makes me wonder if the guys in those beer ads ever throw up on their shoes, go into dry heaves in the parking lot while their girlfriends watch, laugh and smoke cigarettes.

Now I'm thinking of those guys who work in those processing factories over in El Segundo. Sometimes I ride on the same bus as they do. They sit in the back and drink tall beers out of paper bags. They shut themselves off so they can do their job better, with less pain. Their faces look hard in the florescent light. Getting ready for the night shift.

He comes home

Drunk

He pays no rent

His paycheck goes to the local cocaine dealer at work

Makes me think that man is an animal constantly trying to destroy himself. On the way up. On the way down. It's all the same. It's slow death. Suicide by degree. Makes me think that those who blow their brains out are the ones who are keen on instant gratification. They want it all at once. They don't want to settle in for the long haul. They don't understand that it's a long, hard road to the bottom. Pain, misery and depression build strength and character. Sometimes some get so strong and so full of character that they go home and beat up their wife and kids. It's the damnedest thing, those kids pick up on that strength and pass it on to their kids. All the men on the back of the bus look like prizefighters who hold perfect no-win records. I wonder if the man in the Marlboro ad ever goes home and beats his woman.

Kitchen light turns on
Roaches go running for cover

The floor is greasy from insecticide
The place stinks
I don't want to touch the food, it's covered with spray
Thinking about girls strung out on junk
Been looking at a book that talks about
Junkie mothers working as whores
Keep the cash flow happening
Feed the habit
Starve the kid
Looking at pictures of dead junkie girls
Shot herself in the head
Into hell
Works
On the floor the roaches die slow
Their legs kick slowly towards the light
The roach mothers expel their egg sack as they die
It's hot out tonight and the roaches are running
I look in the corner
A roach is eating a dead roach
I can see its little head working, chewing
Junkie girls fucking and sucking for junk
Too high to feed the kid
Inhale the spray and think of the dead girl in the picture

This guy was telling me today about this guy who died in his apartment building. The neighbors start complaining about the smell coming from his room. The police are called and they go into the room with the landlord. They find the guy. He's dead, sitting upright in a chair. His finger tips chewed up from rats that had been jumping up and biting them. He told me about a guy he shot once and showed me his pistol that he had named Betsy. He said shooting someone far away was one thing but shooting them close up was another. I would like to spray some people with bug spray and watch them crawl around in circles like the roach. I would like to watch them die like vermin. I don't have friends, I have thoughts like these. Works for the junkie girl. She vomits in your lap. Your semen, some other guy's as well. Blood, insecticide, mother's milk. Too sick to feed the kid. All the dead roaches, all the dead kids. All the dead junkie girls. I light you on fire. Tie me off. Shoot up the kid for kicks. No don't, that's stupid. You don't want to waste that shit on a fucking kid. What are you, crazy? Choke. Burn your skin. Vomit your guts. Kill yourself. Do it. Shoot yourself up. All the way.

I see you, you bastards. I see all four of you looking at me, staring me down. You don't know who you're fucking with, do you? Can't you hear me screaming? I know you can hear me. I shot myself in the head three times tonight. What else do you want from me? I jumped off every ledge you got. I slashed four miles of wrists and I'm still here with you. I see all four of you standing so straight, so perfect. Why do you put me through this night after night? Every night it's the five of us. I abort, you watch. I scream, you don't answer, all you do is watch. I feel like a bug in a jar. I run my hands over you. You're so smooth, so cool. I put my cheek on you. I kiss you. I have never kissed a wall before but it feels good. I love all four of you. You protect me from them. You're the only ones who care about me and my life. I know you don't care when I leave to get food. I'm not like you. I need some things to survive. I wish I could be like you, straight and tall. I am weak and frail. You make me feel loved. They don't. I hate all of them. You are all I have in the world. Do you remember when I went out last night? I went out to get you something. See, I bought you some cloth to wash my blood off of you. Sometimes when I want to shoot myself, I stop because I know that I will get you dirty with my brains. I don't want to splatter my filthy thoughts all over your strength. I love you too much for that. I have seen what their love does. It lies and kills. They kill each other instead of killing themselves. I wish they would all stay in their rooms so I wouldn't have to hear or see them. I bet it must be great to be in solitary confinement in a prison. All that silence and they shove free food through a slot in your door. I wonder if that's the reason people commit crime, so they can get that time in the hole. I sometimes wish that things had worked out differently.

A public bus comes down the street. The bus pulls to the curb at an intersection. The doors open. Several men in suits get out of the bus. Each has a briefcase in one hand and a one gallon can of gasoline in the other. They make a single file line that goes a whole city block. They all sit down. They pour the cans of gasoline all over themselves. The first man in the line pulls out a lighter and lights himself on fire. While he is burning, he extends his left arm out and touches the man next to him on the shoulder, setting him ablaze. That man does it to the man next to him and so on down the line. The boss looks out the window, sees the fire, curses aloud and calls the secretary to get on the phone and start calling up local temporary service agencies. This happens all the time.

They all swore he was a cocksucking faggot. He was the only gay guy in the whole school who anyone knew about. Imagine the terror he felt when they beat him to death in the park over summer vacation. Do you think you could imagine that? About six idiots, drunker than shit and scared as hell, yelling and cursing to cover their fear as they beat you with their fists and lengths of pipe. Imagine the sound of a baseball bat breaking your jaw. They said you tried to pick up Ed's kid brother. The reality is that he tried to pick up on you and he wanted to keep it a secret seeing as how he was one of the most respected athletes in the school. Ed doesn't want to know that his brother is queer. All he knows is that you are and the two of you were together and that's all he needs. All he did was tell his friends that you tried to pick up on his brother and all of his friends came running. They couldn't wait to kill you. They would have gladly paid. Ed is really kicking you hard in the side and he's screaming at you and he's crying at the same time. He's really mad and you know he means it and it occurs to you that this is how people end up dead in broad daylight. You realize that you're going to be beaten to death and there's nothing that you can do about it. Imagine that the last thought that you have is that you're being killed by ignorance. Ed's brother will never tell Ed the truth. He'll move far from town and start over again. Not you, you're dead.

The junkie fixed up some bad shit and died in his room. His body lay face down on the bed. The heat made the body stink up the hallway. The next morning the landlord opened up the door to the room. Without a word, he wrapped the body in the bedsheet and threw it out the window. The corpse fell right into the dumpster just like in a James Bond movie. The landlord held up two fingers and yelled, "Two points!" He threw the rest of the sheets and the blanket and the pillow out after the body. He rented the room a few hours later.

He was pussywhipped. All of his friends knew it and gave him a hard time. He couldn't go anywhere without her inviting herself along. They fought and fucked all the time. He loved her. He wanted to bash her skull in. She made him feel weak. She made him feel like he wasn't in control of his life. He started to hate her all the time. One night he hit her. Mutual disbelief registered on both their faces. He started hitting her all the time. The more he hit her, the more he loved her. He was in love again, in love with her and it felt good. She could sense it. The way he fucked her now, she felt like a new woman. She would go to the market to get food sporting her black eye proudly. She was glad that she had a real man and not some wimp. She had always wanted to meet a man like her father. A man who would beat the hell out of her like her father used to beat the hell out of her mother. Real steady.

Shit. All these junkies. Remember that girl who used to talk so tough about banging up and slamming. She loved to use those words. She thought we were all blown away when really we had seen so many losers like her come down the pike already. Someone should have told her. She used to try to get me to fuck her. I knew how it would end up; it was the typical Hollywood whore setup. She fucks you and then as you're hanging out afterwards, she asks you if she can borrow some money and then she fucks you again if you give her enough and then you never see her again or if you do, she never brings it up like you're not supposed to remember forty bucks. And then you see the way her eyes look and the way her face looks and sometimes you even see the marks and then you know that it's pointless to ask. She's already dead.

You stupid hungry bitch slammer. I like the way your junk ass moves. You walk on junk crutches, broken down, mechanical.

I'm going to drag you over to the television set so you can lose your mind with your ear stuck to the speaker hearing some fucking soap opera as the daydream of a big syringe dick is going in and out of your junkie lipped mouth glued to a skull. I'm going to turn the television up loud. The voices turn you on. You're a junkie phantom suck machine. A television brain and I have no use for your dead word mouth. I'm going to tear your head open and watch all the television and cigarettes fall out. Your existence will be destroyed when I change the channel.

Little boy blue future PCP slinger. Liquor store robber, bitch slapping killer. Takes no shit from you. Stalks 24 hours day. Fills you with fear. First memory: I saw the boy lose his virginity to the man in the parking lot. I heard him scream. I saw the man break the little boy's arms—sounded like dry wood. I watched the blood drip from his mouth. I heard the words, help, mommy and daddy. The man got in a car and drove away. The little boy didn't move. A while later the ambulance came and took him away.

See the violence in his eyes. See the city come down around your ears. Paranoia at one hundred miles an hour. Stinging dirt and hot rain. Beating off in the sink. Thinking about suicide every time. Slapping at flies and needing a shave. Looking for a woman but finding a fight instead. See the violence in their eyes as you walk into the bar. Check out how hard they laugh and drink. Walk home at night broken and alone. Feel so empty that you think you're going to cave in. See the heat in his eyes. See the man argue with his girlfriend and try to pull her out of the cab. Keep walking. Hot night right now, right here. All you have is what you are. All you want is much too much. All you get is so much less.

All you feel is nothing. All you see is darkness. All you know is senseless and all you can do about it is ride.

I've got a knife and I want to talk to you
I've got a prayer and I want to carve it into you
I've got no chance, that's why I'm looking to you
O Lord, ride with me

INCINERATOR

A song from the heart of the one who knows. The fire of hate burns hot and strong inside me. I am the keeper of the flame. You are the disease. I am the soul of truth. The true fire is the fire of hate. I burn because you live. I will put an end to your lie. I will destroy you. I live to destroy you. I will not lose. I will destroy you and always get what I want. Never forget that. Hear my war cry on the streets of your filthy cities. This flame will never cease to burn. It will burn you and your children and so on until you are where you're supposed to be. I am the real rain. I am the one whom your god spoke of. I am here to do the work that he was not mighty enough to do. It's high time and I am the bringer of the truth. I am the back breaker. I am the father-mother destroyer. I am that which you do not want to see because I am that which makes you see yourself. The only fire is the fire of hate. I am the redeemer. I burn until all is clean and pure. **Call me the Incinerator.**

I walk the streets where I live. Everything is filthy. All the walls are covered with spray paint. The ground is covered with garbage. Dogshit in little piles. The people are fat and ugly. Wasteful and slow. Every once in a while someone will put a new coat of paint on the front of a store. Before the paint is dry, the wall will be covered with graffiti. When someone tries to clean the streets, they are covered in dogshit in a few hours. You have had too much for too long. You are the filth. There's not much that can be done with you. You turn everything into a shit-smacked pigsty. People can be employed to clean the streets and paint the walls so you can have something to do as soon as they leave. I think the cleaners should stop coming. In a week you would be dying of septic infection. No one to clean up after you. I want to put litter in its place. I want to eradicate the planet of you. I watch you throw garbage out of your windows. Diapers, beer cans, shit, food, roach eggs. You are walking death looking for a place to die. Look no further. I have come from a lofty height to wash you off the streets. **Behold the Incinerator.**

I like walking heavy on these disease ridden streets. I like walking the streets knowing that underneath my jacket is the perfect solution to any dilemma I might encounter. I look at people differently. I meet their gaze until they look away. I like taking my gun for walks. I do not believe in hope. I do not believe that people are going to some day going to get it together and live in peace and harmony. I don't have time for political correctness. I'm not going to try to talk my way out of a bad situation. I'm just going to shoot the fucker in the face and be done with it. If you're looking for someone to feel bad about the way things are, then you're talking to the wrong guy. I know the fucking answer. So do you. You take shit from these people like it was the law. You're afraid of your rage. That's how people get over on you year after year. You're afraid that someone's going to call you a nasty name. So if you're a "straight" male and another man hits on you obnoxiously, you will not tell him to fuck off because that would be politically incorrect. You don't have the guts to say that it is what it is: sexual harassment. You cover with the bullshit liberal pose of thinking that everything's alright. You'll tell the man who's stabbing you to death that he looks like he needs a hug. **I am internationally known as the Incinerator.**

I went out late the other night to put the electric bill in the mail box. Two men were standing in the way of the box, locked in a deep embrace. I waited until they came up for air and said, "excuse me." I am telling you all the details because I don't want any of you pricks to misunderstand me and say that I'm a homophobe. You shits call everyone homophobic. How boring. One of the guys got out of the way and the other didn't move. He just thrust his crotch at me and said, "Put it in the box, honey." I told him that he should be careful. Why did I say that to him? Because there are some people who aren't hung up in your world of guilt and your fucked up morality plays. The man was one place where he shouldn't have been, and that was in my face. The man on my left said, "I wouldn't talk like that seeing that it's only you here." He leaned into me and tried to kiss me on the lips. I hit him in the mouth and dropped him. I am going to burn down your world. I am going to upset the balance that you have taken great measures to keep. You can say what you want but know that I don't care because I know that you're full of shit and now you're getting called on it. I make you own up to it all at once and the smell hits you like a ton of bricks. You walk around all your life, lying and hiding behind laws and people that you say you hate. I am the one who comes and checks what credit is left in that dirty little account of yours that you call a mind. I hear all your cities begging me to come and take the pain away. You should be worshipping me. Oh wait, you already do. I always win. Remember that. I can't wait for one of you to break into my place again. The last guy was shot in the face and skinned and hung on the front door. You have been fucking around like little pigs in the mud for too long. **Ladies and Gentlemen, it's star time...... The one and only, often copied but never equaled...... the Incinerator!**

The two of them in the bathtub. They grope at each other. The weak sagging flesh. Stinking gas comes from their genitalia. The water turns black. They kiss. They vomit into each other's mouths. The flesh hangs from their bones as they grab. Witches. Devils. Soldiers made of tortured flesh. She sucks me in the summertime. Explosions, napalm. I want to catch all my dreams and mutilate them. I want to make the perfect nightmare. He grabs at the rotting breast. It's over. The black water rises. Come lover, let's go to the bed. Witches. Devils. The fire of love burning. I want you all to burn like I burn. Lizards. Spiders. They fly out of her snatch. She calls me on the phone and tells me that she wants to fuck me so bad that she can taste me in her mouth right now. I think of the fat that hangs off her arms and the way her breasts sag. You and your stinking body. You want it so bad. Your lies fuck each other and you breed little lies. The fat man humps the woman. She wants to vomit when he puts his tongue in her mouth. They are fucking like pigs. They do it with the lights off so they won't be mutually disgusted by the sight of their flesh. They do it fast to beat the stench that makes both of them gag. Their teeth fall out in each other's mouths. Their saliva is old and it mixes into a putrid paste. When I come in with the incineration, it will be the real thing. I'm going to send this world to a better world. You fuck like a pig. You love me. I don't care. Fuck you. Night driven insane. Night driven to suicide. I am the voice that speaks directly to you. You hate me because I see you. You hate me because I'm strong. Find yourself. Do it. Touch your ugly body. **Give yourself to the Incinerator.**

I'm fucking her. No, I'm killing her. No, I'm fucking her. When I fuck her, I want to kill her. The way she makes me feel. So small. So small when I fall out of her and she laughs in my face. That's when I want to kill her. I want to make her understand that she can't do that to me. I'm not small. I'm big, the biggest. I want to fuck her and kill her all the time. I want it all. I know she fucks around on me all the time in an attempt to weaken me. She laughs in my face and tells me that she needs a real man. I want to kill her to stop the disease. I want to kill all of them. I want to see the look on her face when I crush her lying mouth. I have dreams of coming into her room. She's asleep with a man next to her. I crush their skulls with a baseball bat. I slug away until I pass out from exhaustion. I need to feel better about myself. I need to make her pay. I need to make all of you pay. You turn it all into shit so you won't feel alone. That's why you're after me. You put up with the tyranny of the hell you're in but you take it year after year. You make it better for yourself by passing on the torture. If you can own someone else, then you don't mind being owned. I see it now. I know how you work. I don't want to torture you or own you. I just want to wipe you off the face of the planet because you're weak. There's lot of differences between you and me. You sleep when you should be alert. You don't mind the fat that hangs from your withered body. You tell yourself lies and don't mind humiliating others. The only time you feel any power is when you hold it over someone else. You want to dominate but you don't know the first thing about power. You want the scars but you don't want to feel the pain and go through what it takes to get them. You won't be around for long. **Tomorrow's ash covered victory belongs to me, the Incinerator.**

EVERYTHING

This is Everything
Every twisted sinew car wreck love
The sea gives up
Gets thirsty and dies thin and spitting on dry land
That's where Everything takes over
The other night on Lincoln Blvd.
A Mexican man with a bag full of shitty plastic racing cars
Went from store to store trying to sell the garbage
What the hell was he thinking?
I wonder what the man who sold him the cars told him
That he was going to make a lot of friends and get rich?
That if no one bought this crap
He would be stuck with it?
His family was walking behind him
Two filthy children and his carbon monoxide-dulled wife
She was carrying another bag of shitty plastic cars
The rent is always due around here
The sun sets on their weary shoulders
The neon grinds into their skin
Did you know that right now
There is a beautiful woman waiting to talk to you?
Yes, you!
Not a recording either
A real woman
All you have to do is pick up the phone right now
And dial 1-900-TO-DEATH
All across Bullet Town
The image of a smiling woman
Slams men down into the bottle
Loneliness so deep and hard

It cracks the spine to even think about it
This is Everything
All the cities
The long scream
The unsure fragile thread of life
The black man walking down the street
Tattoo on each breast
Yard hard body
Pimp rolling stride
Trying to conceal the fear
The crystal clear knowledge
That he's never getting out of this neighborhood
Besides a trip to prison and the graveyard
He's got it all figured out
So hard
So fierce
So hopeless
This life rips and dismembers
Doesn't care to know how much you bleed
Doesn't want to know your pain and triumph
I heard a man wailing
His voice sounded evicted
"I lost my woman!"
He had been walking the streets
Winding his way through the bars
Stopping to drink and cry
Falling through the sidewalk
Hours later he got his face wall slammed by a cop
Who liked to prey on what he considered subhuman
He was staggering
Looking for someone he thought was his

Like he could really own someone
Somebody should have told him
No woman is yours
No one is yours
Nothing is yours
Thieves prove that
Everyone will leave you sometime
Look into her eyes
The more you love
The more you will taste the blood
The more idle time you will spend with mortal losers
Like yourself
Your woman
Your man
It just doesn't work like that
The proof is splattered all over the walls
Do you see how the streets open up at night?
The trenches of disease and malice
Yes it's right there
Ugly salesman selling cheap ways out
It's like that
Let the scars of all the stars
Rip you up and teach you something
This is Everything
All the poison love songs
The radio is bleeding
They should sell dried blood scraped off the streets
Tell you it belonged to a daytime television actor
You would line up to buy it
I knew this lady
She used to fuck the janitors

In the apartment buildings in my neighborhood
She used to take care of me while my mom was at work
I would sit in the front rooms of basement apartments
Watch black and white television
While she turned tricks!
This is Everything
A wound stitched together by ghettos
The violent promise of inequality
Trails of crime lights compact the dirt into humanity
This isn't an excuse
Just the facts
Save your bullets and your guilt for later
I walk the scar lines from coast to coast
Observing the effects of compression and consumption
Like tonight at the market
2:15 a.m.
Two women trying to put money together to buy
Two wine coolers and a forty ounce
One of them grabs my shoulder
I feel my fist, I cool it
The security guard tenses
Two Crips enter the market
The guard puts his hand on one of his two guns
I purchase and leave
Walking back to my room I watch others watch others
This place makes you watch everyone
You don't know who is going to go off
So you become perpetually ready
For life to become a movie
This takes years off your life
A group of men weave stiff-legged

Out of a bar and down the street
One walks into a light pole
His friends laugh and pick him up
At the end of all this
Your bones will be ground into a powder
Your blood into dust
Your dreams gagged and brutally pushed out the window
To confuse and complicate the air
The blues hit so hard they crack your ribs
Snap your spine
Splatter your brains on the ceiling
Wrap your car around a tree
Drive you to drink
Love, trust and crawl
The man sits in his car
Parked in the middle of the lot
Turns the radio up
Takes a long drink and lets it pass by
No headaches tonight
He can't go home to that thing watching television
The squawking, screeching mistake
That roaring monster he was once in love with
He stays out at night
Drinks alone
She does the same inside
They have not touched without violence
For two years
The kid doesn't come to visit
He's somewhere in Oregon
Fuck it
So I failed

Failed who?

Whatever

He thinks of a twenty year-old night in the jungle scarred by a fire fight that seemed to last a minute but in fact lasted five hours. A night that resulted in a sharp ringing in both ears, uncontrollable shakes, constant dreams of his best friend's brains cooling on his face.

This is Everything

Because I think that I am going to break

Because I question the ground beneath me

Life cripples and distorts

I can't keep it to myself anymore

Believe me I tried

For years I kept it locked up

Stoic, like a father

Now I breathe cancer and my eyes shoot deathrays

My back wants to break from the weight

All the dazzling beauty

The things that make you want to touch

The urge to destroy what you cannot possess

What you cannot ruin

Because it's out of reach

Because it intimidates you and seduces you into acts of brutality

The stranger rears its head

You see the real thing as you break her jaw

As you rape her

As you rape them

As you crush your hands in your fists

Over and over

All night long

Waiting for the next day to bring you something better than
today
See it in yourself
The focused desperation in your smile
I love you
Don't hurt me
Touch me
Go in me
I trust you
I like you
Please
Don't rape me
Everything told and sold
At the market tonight: A Crip walks with his girlfriend through
the aisles. The Crip is dressed down, heavily built. They discuss
what cereal they should get. I am making jokes to myself about
if they got into an argument, which one would draw first. I hear
yelling at the front of the store. The guard greets another Crip as
he walks in. This Crip is short and built like a tank. He's wearing
gloves and a blue cap. The first Crip sees him and they yell at
each other until they get close and then they shake hands. The
girlfriend and the guard come over and talk to him. I listen to the
short Crip say that this will be the first Christmas he's seen
outside of prison in three years. The guard says he remembers
when he went in. The two Crips fuck with the guard about how
he isn't a gangster anymore. I walk by them and all talk stops.
They look at me. I get my food and get the hell out.
When the world ends
How will I know?
Will there be a sale?
Will they announce it on TV?

Extinct
Everything must go!
Has it ended already?
The stark and unflinching reality
That blows the brains out of Vietnam vets
Keeps me wrapped tight and looking at your hands
Distrusting your every word
Monitoring your every movement
The world ends for some every night
They pull it down screaming
Trying to make it all die
So they can sleep for awhile
I saw an article about people who live in by-the-month hotels off
highways all over America. The article says that they usually
work at truckstops. One guy lives alone with his dog. He cooks
food at Denny's during the day and drinks a case a night in front
of the TV and passes out on the couch and goes to work in the
morning. He says the dog is his only friend and he's been living
there for seven years.
Anywhere you hang yourself is home
It's hard to talk to you
I never get to certain words
Words that would save me
Words that could stop the pain
This is Everything
My life
The wounds
The flickering lights and the fear of mortality
The reason I don't talk to you and never want to see you again is
that you will never know my world. You have yours and I have
mine. It's that simple. All the time you wasted trying to get close

to me makes me hate you all the more. I don't feel that bad about it. If you want to know the truth, I don't give a fuck because you're just like all the others. You're a typical, lying piece of humanity. Like I could ever talk to you. I will never forget your blank stare, your total lack of life. That vacant, faraway look that I mistook for depth and understanding. I bet that somewhere, some asshole is pouring out his heart to you right now. He's hard at it, wasting himself on you, giving you Everything. That's what you want.

The old woman

Throwing the pieces of newspaper she doesn't want onto the street

These pieces of shit never cease to amaze me

The way they mutate and believe Everything

I am one of them

One of the biggest believers

I am a sucker

When I was growing up

I wanted life to be like the shows I saw on television

The mother and father in the same house

They didn't fight

The children were happy

They had friends to play with

Mother didn't scream and chain-smoke

The kids didn't want to kill her

They didn't want to die, they didn't fall behind in school

They were able to control their violent urges

Father didn't come into the room at night

To confess and terrify

The silent rage has built up

Like interest in the bank

You know how it is
When you want to do right
Everything gets in your way
You swing like forgotten meat
On the barbed wire that surrounds the prison camp
You wonder how you let it go this far
As you watch the blood flow from your wounds
And fall with excruciating anonymity
And after a few nights, even that stops causing pain
Regret follows and hollows you out. Rips you off and leaves you cold. It's hard to take. You want to wreck everything in sight. Mindless destruction is the only thing that makes sense. You go for long walks to try to shake it off but you know it's no good. It's all shadows, memories—things that are lost and dangling in front of you. They stick it right in your face and then without warning, they take it all away and it all becomes something that happened. Something that will never return, yet will not leave you alone. What a crime, when you can't leave yourself alone. You look in the mirror, trying to find your friend and you don't find anyone you recognize. The friend you had in yourself is long gone. It's not the same as it used to be. It all changed so fast. It all fell apart, hell it seems like it was yesterday. You have to cover up, deny, run like you're hunted. You are being stalked. This is a new age. It took me so long to see it. For so many years I was looking for ways to kill the pain. I looked in all the wrong places. I assumed that I was alive to a certain extent, but now I see that all these cities are dead beyond belief. Still I go on. I am beyond questioning why. I have a purpose. I tell the story. This is my job—to tell Everything. Until all the skulls are decaying in the street. Until the bones are soil and the blood has dried black into the pavement. Look out when you walk the streets now. I

think there's something in the air. It's making them all crazy.
Don't tell anyone I told you. Also, they stole the sun and put up
a fake one in its place, it doesn't burn as brightly as the real one
did.

That's alright

I'll burn for you

Everything

Coming up on 2:00 a.m.

Sleep is out of the question

The pair of gunshots in the alley tonight sounded like cannons

I am a typical idiot

I went right out there to see who was shooting

A high caliber firearm ten feet from my window

Instinctual death drive

"Drive by? Where?!"

Tonight I wanted to walk

Too late for that

I have come to hate the daylight

All the human war noise drives itself to the brink

Holds its own head under water and tries to kill itself

Unsuccessful, it becomes enraged at its will to live

Have you ever thought of running away?

I don't know where to

If you could take the present reality

And throw it off like a coat

Duck under the wire, get out of the bullshit

And learn a new language

If you have been driven to that edge

To where you're tired of spitting out the same words

Making the same excuses to the same fakes

You have to wonder if there's anything else to life

If you're too smart for religion
And consider prison slightly worse than your current job
Or marriage
Then what do you do?
Everything takes its toll
Because Everything takes its time
Everything's leeching chokehold
Becomes the weight that pulls you to the bottom
Keeps your feet on the ground
And lets you know you're real
This is Everything
It's party time
Think about the absurdity of a heroin party
What games would you play?
What the fuck would you talk about?
"I'm high, drooling and I want to puke."
"Me too."
Partyin' now!
This girl used to write poetry and shoot dope
She went to a party
Took a big dose of smack
This was a heroin party after all
She passed out
Her fellow partyers dragged her into the corner
And kept partying on and on until the break of dawn
They thought she was asleep
She had been dead for hours
The dealer didn't want to call 911
Who needs trouble?
Some party
She told me once

That she wasn't the kind who liked to fight
She'd rather take the abuse
It's all she knew
Her death makes me hate cowards
You have no fucking style
You talk so much shit and you're nothing but slobs
Desperate lemmings dashing off the edge for Everything
Whether you want to be or not
I don't believe in fate or destiny
I believe
In various degrees of hatred, paranoia and abandonment
However much of it that gets heaped upon you doesn't matter
It's only a matter of how much you can take
And what it does to you
I don't know you
But I know you're going to get yours
We all do
And that is the only perfect thing there is
You will get your custom-made hell
And if you blame anyone else but yourself
We'll all know that much more about you
Imagine the horror of the young man who has to leave home because if his father hits him any harder, any more, he's afraid that he will die before he reaches seventeen. He runs away from Seattle to Los Angeles. He leaves all his friends, his sister and mother behind. He didn't have the nerve to tell them that he had to split. His sister freaks when she finds out. She's twelve and she has no one else to talk to besides her brother. She can't talk to her mother. The bitch is always drunk and terrified of her husband. So yeah, the boy comes to LA and he has to get some work so he can have a life. Like you really expect to be able to

come to a city like LA and think that you're just going to walk right in with no formal education and get a job where you will be able to afford a place to live. Get off the drugs and get back to the real world. It can't be done. So it's been a few months and he's getting good at not vomiting every time he sucks some guy's dick down on Santa Monica Blvd. One night some man broke his jaw and left him knocked out in the back of a 7-11 parking lot near Mansfield and Santa Monica. He got himself to the hospital and they ran a blood test on him. HIV-positive.

Tonight is pure
We sleep in blood
Land of one thousand rapes
Someone tore their eyes out in a fit of rage
Mailed them to a country he had never been to
Wanted to see something different
When will they have enough?
When is the last drink
The last drink?
When you wrap your car around something that doesn't move?
When you know that it's the end of the line
Sounds like a good time for a drink
You think this will stop
That someday you'll wake up as if this life were a dream
And you'll be able to deal with it
All the pieces will fit together
As you clutch your crystals and believe harder
All will be just as you thought it was
You'll feel so smart
You knew all along
And then like a rock
Everything will hit you

All the hatred unleashed like a volcanic sewer
The hatred directed at yourself
The hatred you give the rest of us
Thanks for sharing
Thanks for being there when the scars were just healing
Everything
Did you see Everything?
He thought he did
And then he went to Vietnam
And then he went home
And then he went too far
It was a relief
Broke his wife's heart
Broke his daughter's arm
You can keep taking in the information
Until you're an expert in horror
Until your blood cells start aborting themselves
Everything cutting into you
A great, greasy knife ripping through your mind
Moon, June, spoon
Sucking chest wound

Don't kill yourself tonight. I know it makes all the sense in the world right now. The way life gets to you with its pointlessness. The way the others treat you. I didn't think they could be like that either. It tripped me out too. Please don't do this. I want you to stay on the line with me, ok? No, I'm not going to call the pigs. It's just you and me on the phone. No really, I do want to talk to you. Yes, I know I don't know you. Why did you call the hotline if you didn't want to talk? Right, so tell me what's on your mind. What exactly does your mother's boyfriend do to you? Have you told her about this? How many times has he touched you? Have

you told any of your teachers at school? What? How many times
did he burn you with the cigarette? No, please don't hang up. Ok,
try to call back after he leaves, ok? Ok? Hello?
Everything
Every institution of torture
Every beating burning
Ritual spiritual marital
Confessional professional
Process rite of passage
Coming of age at nine
Watching mother fuck different men weekly
Lying to father weakly
When you see him on the weekends you have to lie
Otherwise he goes apeshit
"No, she is alone. She doesn't see anyone."
Don't ask me any more questions
You'll leave me no choice but to tell you Everything
And after a few nights you'll want to leave
And then I'll have to tie you to a chair
And I would do that to make sure you heard me
So, leave now or stay all the way until the end
Still with me?
Wouldn't have it any other way
At the store tonight
I heard the pig tell the rent-a-pig
About the body they found two blocks from here
Shot twenty two times at close range
I walked back, thinking about what that would look like
How you would have to feel to inflict that kind of damage
That's passion
That's real like love

Pure like hate

The streets were clear tonight

It was a few hours before the start of the new year

You might think that everybody was out at a party

I think that they were smart

Staying the fuck off these streets

Like you really need to get shot on your way back from the store!

Like you really need to see your friend lying face down on the ground with a gun stuck in the back of his head. The sight so numbing that you forget that you're on your knees and there's a gun barrel hitting you in the side of your face.

Like a....

What?

Like a sex machine!

Yeah!

Doin' it you know!

Yeah!

Can I count it off?

Count it off!

Bang

Bang

Bang

Bang

Tonight a pig chopper flew so low to the roof that the floor was shaking. I thought it was the mothership, the thing was so loud. I watched it hover. Why doesn't someone shoot these fuckers out of the sky? We'll all be fossils in the street soon enough. Can you imagine taking a walk and seeing rotting corpses and bones of human beings in the gutter? That would put things in a different light, don't you think? Seeing dogs fight with drunks for the arm of a dead girl. Fossils in the street, all teeth picked for gold fillings. Wallets made of human skin. Instead of wearing snakeskin boots, you could use your aunt.

Everything

How many diseases can you count on that man's face?

Humiliation

Shame

Rage

How much more can you take?

I think you can take it all

I think you can take Everything

I can't leave you hanging

I have nowhere else to go

No one to talk to

No one to tell the story to

No one to tell Everything to

I need you more than you'll ever need me

I need Everything

I wish I could exhale it all out of me

Yeah, Everything, all of it

The room strangles and makes a fool out of me

Takes another nail and pounds it into me

I found out Everything about her

Months after she left me alone

Heroin

All the men she hung up and twisted

People call her the Dragon Lady

She fucks and then fucks over

The first part was the most interesting

The second part was the most lasting

The scars still burn red signals

I thought I saw her in a restaurant the other night

My ears, nose and mouth started to bleed
Everything like a plague on your senses
Human overload
In hotel rooms I die nightly
I see brains on the walls
So many nights I have shot myself in these suffocation chambers
Nights spent without breathing
Nights spent living between the lines, in parentheses
Taking cover in the cracks
Everything comes back to me
Many times I wake up dead
Put on my face and hit the door
I get out and head down Death's highway
Everything waits for me there
I can't tell them anything
But I can tell you Everything
I smell blood on my hands
I can taste the blood in the air
Blood, blood everywhere blood
It's rich and sure
One thousand burning ships sinking in my heart
I am looking forward to walking the last mile
Everything gives me the earth blues
Weak flesh columns watching TV
Plugging themselves into alien machines
Sucking the life out of each other
Stealing and exchanging diseases
I see them sickly
They move like born dead again losers
Searching for that desperate golden failure
Striving to attain crippled status

So they can walk and breathe without guilt
Nirvana attained!
Self-mutilators
Damaged corpses staring at each other
Spitting lies into each other's mouths
Everything, everyone
The every man is a nowhere man
Where are you?
It's you against them
Not us against them
I am one of them
So is your best friend
All you have is you
And who is that?
Don't get dumped chumped
Folded molded diluted and convoluted
Look at them
See what they do
Are you one of them?
Or are you one of you?
Who are you?
Ok
I promise not to kill myself tonight
If you'll let me tell you Everything
I am, after all, your favorite dead man
I would like to be able to say that she broke my heart but I know
better. I broke my own heart. I can't say that she did it and get
behind that statement in any real way. I know too much. The only
one I can blame for my loneliness is myself. Even if I did think that
she did it to me, I wouldn't feel any better. Tonight I was
watching a movie and this actor in the film looked like her when

she had a profile shot. She did not break my heart. I did. I don't
know why I would do something this painful to myself. I wish I
would stop, it's been months now and I'm still hurting myself
nightly. I can avoid it for awhile and then it comes back.
Welcome to the empty age
You made it and boy, are we glad to see you
We need help taking out the trash
It's getting ripe in here
When the sewers backup to your door
And you have to pay off someone to unclog your toilet
When Everything comes back
Blows up in your face and rots
The stench will let you know
What time it is
You don't know what you have until it tries to kill you
You don't know what you're missing until you're in jail
You won't know what happened to your life until it's too late
Tonight she told me that she doesn't like to think
She likes to live in the present
The sex was great
I thought she was deep
She's just insane
Everything never sleeps
There's too many gunshots for one heart
I nearly got into trouble by walking into someone else's trouble
Walking to the store smack into a pig bust
Three 9 mm's out
Frantic pigs yelling with their flashlights on their guns
I can't see your fucking hands!
Like David Lee Roth might say
Three Mexicans on their knees

The colored lights swirling around them
The Mex boys with their hands on their heads
Like statues looking into the night
I was thinking how great it would be to see the pigs get wasted
A carload of good guys drive by and shoot them in the face
Remember Rodney King! Viva la Everything!
Food for thought as I walked through the aisles
When I came back they were all still there
It's hard to keep finding ways to fool yourself
Do your arms ever get tired of grabbing at the gold-plated carrot
That dangles in front of your face?
It's getting harder as you get older, I know
You see how it's all going and a lot of the time
You couldn't give a fuck
Everything has the biggest room in your house
And you feel the bite all the time now
The distance between you and them is growing wider
It's harder to find someone to talk to
Everyone's getting so wrapped up in their own lies
Why bullshit someone else
When you can sit in your own room and do it to yourself?
I told her once that all I was looking for
Was one place to go
One place where I could be understood
She looked at me with the blankest stare I have ever seen
Chalk it up to Everything
You find yourself out on the rails again
In bed with another one of these breathers
A wasted night
You could have spent it alone worrying about something
Sitting in the dark with a plateful of frozen screams

Wishing someone was there to lie to you and next to you
It's hard to keep lying to yourself. To keep thinking that you're going to meet someone who will save your ass from Everything. Do you remember the last time you checked and found that you're the only one on Earth who feels the way you do? In fact, you're the only one on Earth besides me. Yeah, that's how it is. It's you, me and Everything. All these flesh bags, hell I don't know, they scare me. It's as if they're just put here to test the two of us. How many robots have you had sex with? Adult robots are so easy to control. Too fragile though, too easy to hurt. Sometimes it's all you can do, you can't help it. You know why? Too many years of Everything, that's why. Mark my words. You will be seeing blood in the streets every day. Don't think about it. It's robot blood. They're bred for this. They were briefed years ago. Have you ever passed a graveyard and felt like a fool for still being alive? As if all those stiffs who had the good sense to get off the ego trip and die for real have some kind of advantage over you because they got it over with? They're dead; you're on your way. But first, the seemingly endless rites of passage. Test after test. Weld your hand to your morals to keep them attached to you. It's like trying to hold onto a burning eel.
They died of Everything
The eleven year old that gave birth on the news the other night
Great promo
The store owner
Looked into the eyes of the man who held him at gunpoint
His last two words
"Please sir......."
His body dropped dropped dropped
Never meet the eyes of an assassin
Soon it will all be withdrawals

We'll all be addicted to something
If you have nothing to be addicted to
Someone will be sent to your home to get you hooked
There's a 100% success rate
If you've never been good at something
You can be a good tragedy
Everyone wants to hear a good story about someone victimized
Everyone wants to be the center of attention
Even if it's only for a little while
Even if it kills
To get the whole picture
You have to align yourself with Everything
You have to crawl into the body of every dead pig
You have to live an entire life on Death Row
You have to scale mountains and prison walls
To know life is to want to kill it
To kill yourself
Every way you can, as many times as you can
Take as many with you as possible
With the power of depression
New avenues of self-destruction
Will make themselves clear to you
The inbred boy at the restaurant looks at the building
On the other side of a vacant lot one hundred yards away
He wonders about people who get to touch people
He's twenty-two, a virgin without a chance of getting out of there
He's hooked up to all the normal tubes and lies
He believes in God
He doesn't see the enormity of Everything yet
He walks around the shopping mall on Friday night
It's somewhere to go

The lights are on and people are touching
I don't want you to kill yourself yet
I want you to have it all
Like your own body bag
I think you should go get one now
You should teach each other how to dig shallow graves
So you can bury each other
Learn to gut and clean a human body
Soon there will be bodies under cars
In dumpsters
Backyards
Families getting together
Dragging father
Who was shot by pigs
To the park
To bury him and the body bag
Bums in alleys under two feet of dirt
Or you could burn your relatives!
Like in Tibet
(Oliver says that the feet burn last)
Take the money you save on the body bag and buy some ammo
Burn your father and stay warm
Hell, he's good for something after all!
See how Everything bleaches your bones
Picks the eyes from your head and sends you to work
Addicted
When you finally kick, the room is dark
You're in a bag
You're in prison
You're in love
Follow the trail of broken noses, jaws and dreams

Tightrope walk on human bones
The road leads you straight to Everything
Each one shoot one
Get through this nightmare
Lots of pigs sit in parking lots at night
They eat and have sex with their partners
It's easy to shoot and kill them
You got to get them before they get you
It was a great moment. We were eating outdoors at this place on
Santa Monica Blvd. This pig came up to us and said that we
faggots had to move. John said that we weren't faggots, we paid
for the food and that we were going to eat it. The pig told us
faggots not to get him mad. John stood up and the pig found out
that John was bigger and meaner looking than he thought and
was probably someone you should address as "Sir." Anyway, the
pig saw that he might get his stupid ass kicked and he backed off
in front of about twenty people who started laughing real hard.
There was no way the pig could make it look like anything other
than what it was. Pigs think they're magic until they smell shit
running down their leg after they've been shot. A week later Big
John bit some fucker's ear off right down the street from where
he scared the pig. That was ten years ago. I lost track of him. He's
in the paper today, no shit: John M., 29, 6' 1", 205 pounds, shot
in the neck and chest by a Santa Monica pig in the middle of the
street. The newspaper said right before he got wasted, he was in
a restaurant and he was freaking out, looking at his hands and
yelling, "Satan is here! The Devil is here!" The owner called the
cops and when they came, John left peacefully, but said to one
of the cops, "God will see that you die, pig." A little while later,
John was spotted near the pier where he threw the security
guard off the side of the overpass. After that John proceeded to

a McDonald's down the street and punched out a female customer. He proceeded east on Colorado Blvd. and at some point he walked into the street and attempted to pull a motorist out of his car. A cop arrived on the scene and John went at him and the pig had to shoot him four times to bring him down.

Shoot a pig in the face for John

Drill your eyes out

Pull your teeth out

Swear off television

Hold your breath

Wade through Everything

Get to the secret place and tell me your best lies

It takes you awhile to see how much your parents mutilated you

When you're too old to change

You'll see that they wrecked you at the beginning

I see it now

You want to kill them

But when they're old it's like drowning puppies

Like I really want to waste my lunch hour

Taking my father out to the sidewalk

To break his skinny arms

So Joe and I went to the place that the newspaper talked about, the place where the pig shot John. We walked Colorado Blvd. thinking that maybe there would be a sign of the shooting, a drop of blood that hadn't been hosed away, something. We walked east. In the middle of the sidewalk, there was a dried pool of blood. Blood all over the place, all over the bushes. We stood and looked at it for awhile. I picked some leaves with John's blood on them and we left.

Do you think that Everything will get so huge and overwhelming

That no one will be able to afford houses?

I see all these bums in the parking lot of the market
It seems like there's more of them every time
Soon all the houses will be boarded up
Everybody will be out on the streets
You'll see dead bodies everywhere
It'll come to the point where the smell of death
Won't even put you off your food
You'll have tasted human flesh
You'll have murdered someone, maybe a few
Imagine an accountant losing his home. He takes his wife and
family into the street. Soon he's fighting a man for a rotten apple
in the parking lot of a market. Other children are beating his kid.
His wife has been raped. He is hopelessly insane. Fear and
desperation are everywhere. The police are stormtroopers who
don't speak to you personally. They just bark easy to follow
orders in monotone. You can get free food coupons if you have
a good body and a way with sex. If you don't think it will come to
this, stick around.
The man at the pier
Looking for work
Not free money
He had his gardening tools with him
He said it's easier to find one hundred dollar bills in the street
Than it is to find work
The whole world will be singing the blues soon
That's all there is for me now—Death
I walk with Death everyday
Death is behind all my hellos and handshakes
I'm choking on Death and breathing deep
Its steady hand on my shoulder
I feel good

Death makes me feel like I don't need anyone
I can sit in this room and wait for Death
To take me out on the highway and up to the river's mouth
Everything has a deal with Death
Kind of like a group rate discount
You're going to die
Not like your parents either
Yours will be like science fiction
They might waste you so they can make a movie out of it
Call it *Sucker: Death of a Mortal*
A nine hour flick about a man that works a job for thirty-five years
In the end, he dies with the gold-plated watch in his teeth
His last words:
"I wanted Everything and all I got was this watch. Damn."
The smell of Death never leaves his nose
Been back from the jungle for twenty years
All the beer and cheap narcotics
Bought from nervous high school students
From here to the coal mines behind his house
Can't wash out the taste of human life burning
The only people he can talk to are others like him
Screaming sweat-filled dream ripped murderers
Totally destroyed by Everything
Everything has so many heads coming out of its neck
So many by-products
Buy products
So many ways to go into an endless downward spiral
The smell of brains
Brains in your lap
Shake the glass out of your hair and talk to the pig
Your friend in the passenger seat is but a memory
Can you believe that you crashed your car?

On your way to the hospital
You smell the aftershave of the attendant
You wonder if it's real or a dream
Nothing like mortality to make you feel alive
I see all the cracks in all the faces
Nothing gets by me
Because I am filled with Everything
Pack glass into my eyes
All the mirrors turn against me
I'll never be there for you
I'll always let you down
Just like hope and life itself
The biggest cons
Have you ever seen someone and thought that they were dead
even while you were speaking to them? They're breathing sure,
but you know by now that has nothing do with it. The living dead
walk the streets, so high on life. They got od'd by their parents,
their coaches, their bosses. Now they're addicted to Everything.
They never get enough to get off all the way. Their frustration
puts their brain cells in prison cells.
The convenience store holdup
The robbers were dressed as cult heroes
The owner shot them like it was nothing
I saw it three times on the news
Put that to a rock beat and get out there and jack your body
Don't slip
So much blood on the dance floor
He had to move the dairy refrigerator to clean it all
My neighborhood smells like bug spray and Death
How about yours?
It's a bloated fucking joke

But you'll take it every time
You'll pray to it
Fall prey to it
You'll believe it every time
You're good
One of the best
I know a guy who talks a lot about forgiving people and finding
the way to love them. He knows it's there and it's just a matter
of guts to find that way. I think that's a crock of the most
succulent bullshit. I will never be close to some people. I don't
think about them except when one of the scars starts to swell. All
is fine until the rage starts to make life harder than usual and
then I can't find a way to love anything and I just want to see all
of you shiteaters die. Shoot you and your gods right there in the
parking lot. Put your fucking brains in with your Big Macs. Hack
and keep hacking. If I walked up to you and shot you in front of
about ten of your friends, it would help them. If I never asked
your name because to me you're all the same, that would help
your friends out immensely. They would see what I see, that it's
all cheap. Worthless. And that we're all modern gods. It's all
eight o'clock television. Anyone can be a fat piece of shit come-
dian and make millions aping their stupid white trash heritage to
the amusement of those who somehow find themselves above it.
When your brains are on the hood of your car, they'll see it all.
They'll see Everything.
And then Everything makes the rounds and stops by your place
Your friend gets wasted by a piece of shit
Shot in the face on your front steps
The neighbors never saw anything
They talk shit about you to the newspapers
They live in fear

But not as much as you

For you the nights come with nightmares free of charge

You lost more than your friend

You lost part of yourself

Earth isn't the same

You get your eyelids peeled back

You never see things the same way

There's only short breaks from the paranoia ache

All the people you know are different

You all have a dead body in common

You associate them with the corpse

They do the same with you

Your life gets ruined by strangers

And now Everything is real real real real

That's usually how it goes right?

They take a little of you away every time you leave your house

You wanted Everything and now you're on your way

All at once you want to pull back

To get away and make it all a dream

Reality becomes a nauseating, horrific constant

Takes the taste out of your food

Takes the joy out of sex

Takes the life out of life

You know there's people out there

Who just don't give a fuck

I mean they really don't

They will kill you

They will never know your name

They won't remember your face

They're cold like you never got a chance to know

We do though

Those of us who have to deal with your body
The sickening strangeness that you take on
Now that you're something that has to be disposed of
Life was hard enough with depression and taxes
You never counted on someone you know being murdered
My streets are filled with rent boys
Hollywood nightmares hanging out
Standing in the middle of the sidewalk
Kings and queens of the shit pit
Making money with their assholes
Some have guns
The neon snarl of the whore hotel
The whores sitting in the lobby
The shit-talking white boys outside
Smoking and scratching their legs
A man's head was found in a parking lot a few blocks from here
I don't go outside much at night anymore
I am one of those people who knows that shit happens
Everything has come this way
Overflowing
Overwhelming
Overloading
The circuits are blown and everybody's sick and scared
Even the plague is getting tired of being so mean
But it doesn't know what else to do with itself
All the new dictionaries do not include the word *mercy*
But this is Everything so let's get on with it
At the end of all of this
At least we'll be able to say that we were able to face some of it
Without wanting to puke or shoot ourselves in the mouth
I can only speak for myself

I have my hand on Poison's pulse
It's strong and steady
People I know
Are now people I knew
They got taken back there somewhere
Taken into the dark and beaten with hard life blues
Now look at 'em
Fish out of water all the time
Mean and getting closer to a grey skin ending
Everything blocking the sun
Sucking the heat from your bones
Making them all liars
You desperately clutch for animal skin
Time rips you off
As it goes whoring down Knife Street
I live in this hot room and I wait for the gutted night
I know then where I should be
Behind the locked door waiting
Lights, camera...
Shoot a pig in the face!
Rodney King's pig-bull attackers are going to go free
It's not enough to have a pig beating on video
The pigs still go free
Now we know without the slightest doubt
(We foxhole dwellers never had any doubts)
The pigs run this town
Hey shithead, guess what?
You have no voice
No rights
No life
Tonight LA County's flesh is burning

Only the lean tissue
The ghettos are incinerating
Beverly Hills is as serene as a Christmas carol
Plastic angels with NutraSweet wings
A broken window in Westwood
The flesh burns and peels off the back of the beast
It howls and begs
The history books will become flesh
The pages will scream forever
It will all be nightmares
The pages will raise the bruises of ten million beatings
Beatings that happened before your ears could hear
Hate is now genetic
Rage is in the heritage
The children will be born with tear gas scars on their tiny lungs
Price for slavery
Small price to pay for Everything
Outside you can smell the flesh burn
Smells like the hair on your mother's neck
On fire
It's all that's on the news right now
The pig chief with his barely concealed erection
I kept watching his face as he spoke to the cameras
I wanted to see his head explode from the sniper's bullet
Tonight is a night for bloodshot moon-eyed poets
Crack smokers can watch their hovels burn
The ghetto eats its own tonight
Another night into the now famous LA riots
I watch the stores down the street burn
All you can smell is smoke and failure
Centuries ago

Central American tribes sacrificed people all the time
Captured enemies
Young girls
Anything to keep the gods happy
And the good vibes flowing
Wait a minute
Those guys were primitives
Savages
Running around killing people
Nothing like us
Make a volcano
Feed it pig bodies as a sacrifice to the gods
Fuck it
We'll use Dodger Stadium
Take all the pigs and their families
All their guns, cars and choppers
Sprinkle with a few tons of Napalm
It'll only take a few days to get rid of the problem of crime
And then Everything will be fine
But it's not that easy
As you sleep
The pigs are getting stronger
They smell their own fear, they mutate
And get higher than you do even with all that dope you smoke
You stoned fuckup
They use your heads to climb higher up the pig ladder
The more I think about it, the more I think Kurtz was right. If he could have seen how the shit has piled up on the streets, how civilization has decayed... Maybe he already had seen it and had seen too much. I stay off the damn streets. That's just how it is. I don't trust them. I don't like them and I don't know them. I'm not

looking for lightning to come from the sky anymore. I no longer believe in storms. I see a life ahead of beating the numbers, beating the stats. Getting through the maze and taking cover. There's no room for thought here. It's all been reduced to instinct. I've gotten good at running low in parking lots and keeping out of the line of random fire. I want to die clean. I don't want to get taken out by a guy whose neck I could break with my hands. I don't want to die with one of the last words coming out of my mouth being "Sir." I don't want to beg on the way out. A pathetic slob with some Pavlovian knee jerk reaction of wanting to live now more than ever since there's a man sticking a gun in my mouth. The only way to control your destiny is to get a gun and even then all you stand is a chance. The only other thing you can do now is to go way up river. So far that you lose your mind and the dreaded Everything that came with it. Pull back into darkness one more time and contemplate your shaking little life. Some people just don't care. Their fear is bigger than yours.

The small-eyed insect man came at me

He tried the tough guy routine

He had no idea

What he was fucking with

You have no idea what you're fucking with

Some people are more than people

They are forces of nature

They separate themselves simply

By the fact that they kill

They know there's no magic involved

Some are only afraid of doing time in prison

That's all

After that they have all the fear of a shark

Tonight I saw a man using a public phone

Receiver in one hand
Cock in the other
Pissing onto La Brea Ave.
I watched the couple advancing a few feet away
They were in for a surprise
Things like that bring us closer
Do rapists ever get birthday cards from people they raped?
Sometimes life is one endless rape fantasy
Finally you give in and get into it
That's how they sell you Everything
Take a second and think
All the poison you take in
For the sake of wanting to belong
City-grade strength
Is determined by your tolerance to poison
How much you can take
City dwellers come to resemble roaches
Years go by and they can take more and more poison
It's called *making it*
The horror rings dull in your ears
Keep choking
Keep working
Keep on mutilating yourself
There's only one way not to get hurt
And that's to be the one who delivers the pain
Install fear into their minds like a component
Deliver it like a newspaper
The streets are paths of human pain
He pulls out of the parking lot after shooting his friend
Drives the four blocks home
Shoots his wife and then himself

He was tired of being hunted
Sick of the bitterness and paranoia
He said the same thing to the two he dispatched
"You're welcome."
You know that saying, "It takes all kinds." It only takes one kind
to ruin your life forever. The kind that keeps you distracted and
looking over your shoulder for the rest of your days. That's the
kind they make all the movies about. You get to watch the worst
situations while you sit in the comfort of your breathing skin.
The real thing is different. The pigs in the movies never act the
way they do in real life. In the movies, they're almost human.
They never get the LAPD pigs right. It only takes one kind to
make all those other "kinds".
Celine said there were two distinct races of people
Rich and poor
There's two kinds, that's for sure
You and them
Poor LA cop
Suffering from Posttraumatic Stress Disorder
How the fuck can I care?
If you can't handle it
Don't take the fucking job tough guy
Do the right thing
Kill yourself
Don't go on television and tell the world
That you're all torn up
Just go into the living room and die
You're a pig slave to the king of pigs
In LA, the town where America has gone
To get smaller noses, bigger tits
Darker skin, lighter hair

And shot by teenagers with names like "Little Ghost"
You treat people like objects of disgust
And then you act like you're spiritually wounded
When the same gets done to you
They should build a memorial wall in LA
Like the one in DC
Instead of Viet dead
It would be dead pigs
New names popping up all the time
At the end of each summer
A new panel would have to be added
It would become a great party spot
You could go to laugh at the crying boyfriends, wives and children
Yeah, it's gotten that bad
I know I've had enough
Everything has gotten to me
I know I'm not the only one out there
One in a million million?
No way
If I was the only one who hated pigs
LA wouldn't have burned to the ground
People wouldn't have been outside the courthouse
No one would have.....
Fuck this
I nearly fooled myself into believing
That I had something in common with one of them
Someone who poisons themselves with alcohol and television
Temporary full-of-shit-ness on my part
Reach out and feel the real coldness of human nature
Want to learn about your fellow man?
Study the insect
Watch how they breed, die and kill

Feed and fuck
For nothing
Endless human mutiny
Alas
We are stranded
Desperate
Sometimes when the bullets are asleep in the chambers
I look out the window and listen to the traffic
We fucked up
How some people can be in so much pain
That they will kill themselves
That tells me the story of Everything
I stagger through the nights
Reeling from it all
Constantly recoiling from reality
Reading the papers
Turning pages
Repeating the mantra under my breath
Sports crime weather war
Sportscrimeweatherwar
Sportscrimeweatherwar
Sportscrimeweatherwar
Avoiding Everything because I know it will kill me
Because it's terrifying
Wondering if you could meet someone who could take it away for awhile. Wondering if there's anyone out there who could hold you and not have their arms fall off. Someone who wouldn't shoot themselves in the head as soon as you told them your life story. You hold it in long enough and all of a sudden, you find yourself loading people into a walk-in freezer and shooting them in the head.

Sportscrimeweatherwar
It's a matter of balance between
The truths you don't like
And the lies you can live with
The ones you use to insulate yourself from the truth
Most of the things that you think are true about yourself
Are the flattering lies that others tell you
When they come out of the mouth of someone else
They're true enough
It's how you keep breathing and get to work on time
Drink your way around the rough edges
Neutralize yourself until the truth smoothes out
And cuts you a little slack
Let the television hold your shaking little hand
Because it's better than real life
The shit outside that fills you with fear and rage
Forget the therapist
Get a box of shells and a fifth
I see it everywhere across this battered and scarred plane. The
doors are unlocked because all the buildings have been burnt
and looted already—nothing left to take. All you can do is take
your hate home (if you have one to go to) and let that burning
lump of unending fury keep you occupied until the next riot
starts. Some malt liquor company should have done an ad
showing a tired human coming back to his 'hood after a tough
day of rioting and looting. He expends his clip into the air and
lifts a cold 40 oz. bottle of the stuff to his lips while behind him,
a strip mall burns out of control. For all the fucked up shit they
do, this Everything's for you.
If the planet could make a sound
I think it would be a scream
A scream mixed with coughing and spitting

It would sound like dropping chunks of volcanic glass
Into a combine
The news spends more time than ever on local crime reports
No more weather
No more sports
No more war
Wars take too long
These people in the East, what losers
Fighting wars that are centuries old
Dad, your sons want a war they can call their own!
Should gays be allowed in the millitary?
SHOULD ANYONE?
Soon the news will just be crime
New crime
Crime Television
CTV

Thirty to sixty minute installments of bad black and white footage of cashiers getting shot behind the counters of gas marts. Composite drawings of Death Row-eyed men who did things to other humans in towns with forgettable names. Movies will no longer be about crime and funny cop teams shooting people every ninety seconds. They'll be about sports, weather and war. Normal business men and students will be able to sing all the words to gangster rap albums and say that it reminds them of themselves. Everyone alive will have killed someone else to still be breathing. Gang members will be mad because everyone will have all the same fire power and kill stats as they do. Everyone will be gun carrying, conservative (terrified) homicidal citizens. Then what?

Everything, that's what
That which cannot be stopped
That which will disintegrate the history books

That which will render your childhood obsolete
So numb
That when your friend passes out
From that junk overdose
You turn the channel on the set
Look over at the cooling stiff
Smile and say
Good stuff
We're all tripping from too much junk
Everything you touch
Gives you a contact high
And a hangover
You look for the hair of the beast
Who broke your back and filled you with poison
Who stripped you of your will to live
Who made you a porno-fueled rape addict
You get raped all the time
Music
Pigs, government, morality
Sportscrimeweatherwar
They fuck you with your own fear
They get you on your back so often
That a jury might conclude
That you like it
That you won't mind paying for more
That it's all you know
And in some strange way
It's all you need
Anytime, anywhere
Tourists coming into Miami, Florida
Get robbed in their rental cars

The German lady
She left so much blood
On the pavement
Of the bitchinest little continent ever
That it spilled onto four different channels
I saw the atrocity shows, one after the other
Interview with the seventy-two year-old rape victim
Everything isn't enough anymore
There's so much
It all turns into a bad nightclub stand-up act: "So the girl comes
out of the bar and she's walking to her car. At the same time, six
guys walk out of a topless bar and see her. One of them grabs her
and slams her into the side of a truck. He rips her blouse open
and tears her skirt off. He punches her in the face and tries to
rape her as his friends just stand and watch. Are you with me so
far? Ok, so she's trying to get away and he slams her against the
side of the truck and breaks her thumb and three of her ribs. His
friends urge him to leave. As he walks away from her he says,
'I've always wanted to do that to a bitch.' Get it? Hey what is this,
are you all dead out there? What is this, an Elvis Presley post-
mortem look-alike contest? Saul, get me out of here. These
people are deadbeats!"
You might surprise yourself after all this
Sometimes it takes a crisis
To make you see what you're really made of
Maybe a life of paranoia and dull, numbing fear
To make you see
That this place really isn't so great
Do you remember when you were younger, you used to run
around and play inside old fucked up buildings? It was so great
because it was wrecked anyway and you could do whatever you

wanted, which usually meant break anything that was still standing. You liked the place because it was part of their mess, the wreck of the people before you. These unknown people from a generation who had nothing to do with your life. For many years you could go through the streets and not care that the place was falling apart because it was theirs. Their streets, their buildings, their mess, their Everything. You had no idea why it was all falling apart. It was their problem. All you had to do was run around and yell and scream and get home in time for dinner. You could laugh the whole thing off. Now things have changed haven't they? Now it's your problem. You inherited all the mistakes and all the ideas that didn't work and backfired. Too bad that the blast burned your face and not the ones who schemed the whole thing in the first place. It always ends up like that though, doesn't it? The backlash is all yours. All the bottled rage and all the condensed fury. All the ruin and decay that we were able to distance ourselves from has now changed its appearance. It seems more familiar. It bears our face and our characteristics. All of a sudden, it's us, it's ours. Now we watch children run through the ruins of our collected failures. No one takes the time to tell them that they don't stand a chance. We become fossilized while still moving.

You're the first, the last, my Everything

Johnny Mathis on PCP: *Look at me / I'm as helpless as someone cuffed and getting gang-raped down at the station / I'm fucked up / Like a murder witness being held over night in a room full of pigs / I'm so lost / Like an uneducated man trying to not become a criminal / I'm nothing without you...*

Tonight I saw a big roach

It was under the rim of the toilet

Eating something

A roach dining
On something you couldn't even think of surviving on
You don't stand a chance
Think about it
Think about Everything
Think about the ones who tell you that you're not doing your part when you tell them that you have decided to go in a different direction than the one they have chosen. They'll tell you to stop screwing around and get serious. Get to work. Get one of those jobs that ruins your back and obliterates your self-esteem. A job that reduces you to a stooped idiot filled with nothing, trippin'. They fucked up didn't they? All they can show for their lives is the fact that they don't mind the feeling of the bit in their mouths. They've been getting yoked by the reins for so many years that they've become proud of themselves for being able to take the pain for so long. It's the only thing they have left besides bills and regret. Imagine being proud of how much pain you can take from a stranger who is richer than you are. Life is full of humiliation. Some get addicted to it. When you go your own way, they see a part of themselves that they swore they would hold onto forever, but instead allowed to atrophy and eventually starve and wither away into complacency before it disappeared and returned full of bitterness and contempt for itself. A life denied living in denial. They have no way of getting it back and they want you to be as miserable as they are so they can have a shoulder to cry on during happy hour.
How do you survive the endlessness?
The weight of mortality bearing down on you
Scaring the shit right out of you
Take your mind off the real world
Go watch rubber tits and dead bodies pile up on the big screen

She was too beautiful to live
She didn't have many lines in the script
But she had great hooters
So she got naked
And then she got killed
Get yourself some of those rubber tits
We don't care if you're female or not
If you got 'em, we can use you
Even if you don't
We'll find a way to use you
Squeeze you in
Flatten you out
Wring all the juice right out of you
Throw in a little rape to keep it all PC
And then shoot you
I watched the pig get interviewed on television. Busted for violating a man's civil rights. As if five men beating a fallen man with clubs is a violation of civil rights and not a violation of some higher ordinance. Something like that has to go to court. Too bad you can't take garbage like this out and dump it. This remorseless, ignorant slob smirked and explained how he was just doing his job and doing it well. Send in a crude man with crude instruments—guns, tasers, and clubs—and all you'll get is crude work. Infuriating to watch this pig, he'll do no time. We'll all do it for him.
I watched a pig pull over a carload of Mexican men
"Where do you think this is... Tijuana?"
Run the warrant check
Hope that they make one move
Break the bones
Hit him with the taser

Electrify
Take a breath
Take a life
Pigs with children
What a thought
Doing time
Lots of thugs
Some with badges, some without
Where do you go?
What do you do?
All of a sudden you're the weak link in the chain
You're the one not pulling the weight
You think you are
That ball and chain feels pretty heavy
If you don't arm yourself, you're begging for extinction
What happens when your kind is gone?
Who will be left?
What will a world of the "fittest" look like?
Guns with legs and credit cards
Tonight would be a good one for the poets
First there was the argument outside
It ended in woman-screams and a gunshot
Soon after the pig chopper came overhead
The god's eye shone down upon me
I was in the pig show!
I felt so special
I felt I had been blessed
But some nights you get lucky
You get to hear the return fire and the chopper blades
Every night like loneliness and silent love
The pig choppers come over me

Visiting pig angels
Extraterrestrials
Oh!
Another night for the poets
Stabbed and bleeding in the city of shitheads
Coming out of the poetry reading club
Smelling the jasmine and car exhaust
They see the choppers too
We're in it together
They serve no purpose
They know people though
They know that the bigger the machine, the more in charge of things their operators look. That's all it takes. You see one of these flying pigs and you got to figure he knows what he's doing. He's flying a fucking helicopter! In truth, he knows nothing more than he's flying *in* a helicopter. That's why there has to be more ground-to-air missiles owned by citizens. Imagine the pig flying over the city wasting time and gas, when he should be shooting himself in the face. He sees a red tracer and that's all he sees. It's all over. On the ground, they are partying like a motherfucker. **R**ocket **P**owered **Gr**enade launchers by mail. What a beautiful idea. RPG Party! It's really the only way to keep the pigs in line. I want equal time. I want to fire tasers into pigs anytime, anywhere. I don't want my MTV. I want my American convenience, bitch! I want to shoot these pieces of shit out of the sky when they come over the roof of the apartment. I want to take them to my station and beat the shit out of them. I want Everything. Because I'm lonely. Because I'm insane and sick and can't talk to people. I try and then the black wall rises and hurls me back into my darkened room. I want her to know me. I don't want to know more about sickness and insanity. I want to stop running. I want her to hold me in her arms. I want to think that she's an angel.

Help me before I turn into still breathing black cancer. Please save me from the Inferno, the Abyss. Save me from myself. I am dangerous to my mind. I'll starve my brain until it's almost dead and then I'll jolt it back to panic life on stronger, darker horror. I'm good at it now. At this point, it's all I know. Besides Everything, horror is the only thing I feel safe with.

I see men pissing in the street every day now

Someone should write a little poem about that

I wonder what the women who work the street in front of my apartment building think about the guy who just got caught with a woman who had been dead for three days in the back of his truck. He claims that he has killed seventeen prostitutes in all. He's given instructions on where to find other bodies and they're turning up. Thirteen so far.

Later in the week he pleaded

Not guilty

At least someone's feeling good around here

I wonder what whores think about when they're getting into cars. If they look for the knife, a quick movement of the client's hand. I wonder if they think about getting killed while they're doing business. I wonder what that kind of constant fear does to a person. Maybe it's like being in prison. Or trying to get elected.

I pass the crackhead woman

She makes a grab for my groceries

I dodge her and keep moving

Another woman asks me if I want a date

Pay

To fuck you?

Darwin would not want to miss a second of this

You want evolution-while-u-wait?

You got it right here

A man can go to Vietnam and end up on the street looking through garbage for a meal while a man with soft hands who never saw anything more intense than a college prank sails by in a limousine. A woman can live in a city park, not use a toilet for three years, get raped, beaten and starved and still survive. We're dealing with a higher human here. This is what Nietzsche had the erection about. This is where it was heading and now here we are. Forget art. Some guy's painting isn't an example of an elevated state of mankind more than a man who shits his pants and screams at the top of his lungs in his sleep. His head full of dead bodies and rice paddies. On the other hand, *you* can go marvel at Jurassic Park and buy a stuffed dinosaur. Excellent! The future?.......

Let's not deal with the problems spitting in our face....

Let's dig up Hitler and kick his goddamn ass!

.....Again

This time we got him!

A movie didn't kill Hitler

He killed himself

Don't you get it?

He won

He completely pulled his mission off

Thought it up and did it

More charisma than ten Reagans

No Hollywood director will never be as widely remembered

Back to the future...

I'm putting my chips on the guy who can eat garbage

And take beatings from the pigs on a regular basis

You don't get pushed hard enough for my liking

I'd like to see the weak get weeded out

I'm tired of having to share the place

They bring it all down so low
These young people on their asses
Begging for beer money
Can't you come up with something better?
Is this the way you're rebelling against your daddy?
The one you said abused you for years?
Can't you do something more creative?
Like blowing him up?
Like outearning him?
Instead of being a filthy, weak piece of shit
Not even twenty
Oh yeah, here's some evolution at MTV attention-span speed:
Take millions of years to get the fish out of the mud and into a
car. Evolution. From living in caves to staring into the night sky
from the top of the Trump Tower. Amazing what people can do
when they put themselves into something. It's not enough though.
We don't need God. We'll do it right here, right now. Crack
Babies. Dysfunctional families giving birth to even more fucked
up, genetically damaged offspring. The genes scream. The DNA
twists in agony at the fact that it is committing an obscene crime
by replicating. Evolution rages madly on. Children beaten in the
womb. Sperm cells stabbed and maimed as they swim frantically
towards the imagined goal. Don't do it! Bail out! More monsters
on the way.
Everything never sleeps
Always out looking for recruits
Like pimps
They always get the runaways
Looking for the daddy they never had
You fucking farm animals. I see you in the shopping malls
dragging your litter of children. The resources run out right in

front of you and all you can do is make more kids. We'll have to go back to the old fashioned, manual, hands-on wars to weed them all out. You fucking bovines with briefcases. What are you thinking? Why do you need a tribe? One child is all you need. Want two? Adopt one. There's tons over at the pound waiting with their little noses pressed up against the chicken wire, looking for a good home. I guess you need more than one to molest and mutilate. Evolution goes on, without judgment...

I think you should be put in cages and set out in the country. Penned in by walls of chain link. Soon there'll be so many that you'll have to kick them out of the house to just be able to eat. Too many people. It's over. All bets are off. You're going to lose them to the bullet anyway.

Give me an E, give me an V.......

Christians are my favorite comedians. Talking that bullshit. Shooting those abortion doctors. Grinning blankly and stupidly into the lenses of CNN cameras. You guys are hot. Dragging your dull children out there with you on a Saturday when all they want to do is get high and fuck... Your conviction and your little signs are meaningless. Squeaks in the wind. Like you could stand in the way of evolution. Like you could ever control life and death.

Look out

You never know when you're giving yourself over

Never know when your throat is exposed

These head feeders

They don't waste any time

Morality breaks down

What can you do against a sociopath?

By the time you sidestep your morals

Your sense of right and wrong

You're dead

You're so tiny
Your little words
Lost in the wind and backwash of siren scream
I see this old man every day sitting on the steps. He watches the
whores on 12th Street. He sits there from early morning until late
at night. Waiting to die while watching the streets rot in front of
his eyes. I wonder if he thinks about evolution as he scopes the
ugly whores work the sidewalk in front of him. The oldest trade
in the world. Yeah right.
I think we should hurry up and get it over with
People who litter are working towards it
They're pushing it right along
Let the garbage pile up
Let everyone see what they really leave behind
In a few days you'll be knee deep
Praying to the president
Natural disasters aren't enough
You need more
You need to have it happen to you
Then Everything will become real
Don't worry because Everything is coming
All you have to do is live
Soon there won't be anyone
Who isn't a criminal or a victim of crime
A good way to get the guns off the streets: Let the assholes start
killing everyone. Pigs stay home. Take the phone off the hook at
the pig station. Just stay home! (And blow your brains out!) Same
with the firemen. The other day some firemen responded to a
call and for their trouble they got firebombed and two of them
went to the hospital with severe burns. On the news, some
representatives said that the fire department held no grudges

against the neighborhood but you knew that those guys under-going skin grafts in ICU were wishing it were the doers. So you firemen, stay in the station when the bell rings. Let the fucking block burn. Most people are homeless anyway. No one will know the difference. After a few weeks of chaos, all the assholes will have killed each other trying to play King of the Shitheads. Sure a lot of innocent people would be dead but at this point there's really no innocent people so the hell with 'em. The streets would look like what we do to countries all over the world. It's time we see what our tax dollars are not doing. I think we would be doing something for the good of the nation. Wouldn't you sacrifice one of your relatives for the good of the nation? How about your next door neighbor?

Keep breathing, human

You watery little digit

Keep walking the streets until one of yours

Kills you

You know that saying, "History repeats itself"? I think it's true. But I think it's quicker than a repeat. It's been centuries of the same, unraveling thing. One long breath. One long first take. From the fuckheads with togas to the fuckheads in suits. You can kiss my ass with your history books too. All that useless paper. "Those who don't learn from history are doomed to repeat it." You can kiss my ass with that one as well. How long does it take to learn about what's been coming in your mouth every minute for the last one hundred years? Those who are alive are doomed to repeat history because a bunch of weak motherfuckers learned how to run the game from their fathers. You can learn about them all you want to but you're going to repeat Everything over and over.

The woman with the paper bag face

Calls me over

She's lying in a doorway
Next to a man who is passed out
The area around them stinks of urine
She wants me to give her money
Keep civilization going for another day
Hold up the crumbling arches
Shoulder the sadness
Climb the ladder of scars
Don't look down
Don't look anywhere but straight ahead
Dead ahead
Ahead is dead
The head is a dead place
It's a killer
The drug dealers have faster faces
Darting eyes
They know how fast it's all coming to an end
They're just trying to get some commerce going
Before everything starts burning again
Another woman with a broken face
Staggers in with a man
She's trying to get him to buy her more beer
They stink and drift
It's good to know that there will always be criminals. You'll never
have to waste your time thinking that things could ever be
better. Crime will never go away because criminality is part of
the heritage. Without crime, the machine would seize and stop
dead on the highway to oblivion. Crime is a twenty-four hour a
day thing. Millions of dollars are invested to make sure crime
runs smoothly and endlessly. Recruits are searched for at all
times. If they can't be found, they are made. Groomed. Criminal-
ity is a way of life. You can't right the wrongs because you'll

never understand the cause and you'll be too busy dodging the effect. You can only suffer the consequences and fear what is to come. Guns don't grow out of the ground. You become a gun-toting maniac to protect yourself from gun-toting maniacs. You use language and morality to make yourself feel better than the people you fear. Don't waste your words. Don't waste time justifying your actions. Just do your fucking thing and get it over with. No one will notice. They're too busy choking on their own fear.

Poison for sale

So much poison

You become a victim

Of those not strong enough to bear the weight of freedom

If you waste any time

Thinking that anything is sacred

You'll get taken out faster than all the other suckers

The burned out hull

Of the Thrifty's market that got torched in the riots

Is already covered with graffiti

Is it just me

Or are the hands of the clock spinning faster?

The endless beauty contest

Who's going to last through to the next station break?

Soon you're going to start tearing down people

Faster than you create them

One day you'll wake up and have nothing to worship

But yourselves

No more Michael Jackson

He was dismantled by the same ones who gathered at his feet

Bill Shakespeare time

It's all par for the collision course

Killers in office
Death Squads on the streets
No more channels to change
Funny how much you adapt to
Please read that as how much you can become numb to
Distance yourself from
And deny
I knew a woman who came from Norway to America
To take photographs of homeless people in LA
The polluted air put her in the hospital for three days
And there you are
Breathing away
Clocking the bodies and checking the headlines
Keep breathing mortal
Future body bag occupier
Commercial believer
Television watcher
It's all yours, Sportscrimeweatherwar
Don't try to separate yourself from the bad stuff either
Tonight I watched the street men make camp on 12th and 3rd.
The group dissolved to two men sleeping with shopping carts
around them like a camp of covered wagons against the throng
of youths talking loud emptiness and drinking out of forty ounce
containers of malt liquor. They slept with the roar going on all
around them. Hours later I came back and looked at them. They
were still in the same position they had been in hours before. But
now they were covered with urine and beer. There was broken
glass from the bottles that had been thrown at them. One of the
men had his shoes neatly arranged next to his head. Somewhere
on the streets of the Village, someone's laughing about how he
took a leak on a bum who didn't even move the whole time.

That's you and your civilization
I look at all of you and that's all I see
When this heap turns to ash, I'll say we're even
I don't even answer to them anymore
These fakes give life a bad name
I have lost my respect for humans
Life is one thing
They are another
Hold up your little picture of peace
I'll hold my little picture too
The one of a dead soldier being dragged down the street
Surrounded by people struggling for a chance
To kick and mutilate him
What status
A divine object of hatred
They all want you
They want to release their hatred
A few kicks to your dead ribs will make them feel better
It's a strange way to worship....
But take it if you can get it
They can do so much worse

I refuse to answer the stupid question, "Where do you see yourself at fifty?" What a joke. Like I can really believe that I'm going to make it that long. There will be a time when death caused by a bullet will be a "natural cause." I don't see fifty years old for me. I know too much. I know Everything.

A homeless man's introspection: "Without solitude, I would be full of their mindless, meandering blur. They move like ants. To myself I think, give them something to fear that cannot be seen so its size escapes the imagination. The fear of God no longer works. These days they own the same weaponry as the police. What then will keep order amongst them? Heroin in the tap water? How brilliant they are in their cruelty. How unthinking in every act. Almost instinctive. The city defines them. They get their morals from their paychecks, their information from their televisions and their wisdom from movies starring Tom Hanks. What will become of us?" Three days later he's dead in the park. Frozen solid. No one to ID the body. A report shorter than a grocery list goes to the city M.E. The "Special Remarks" part at the bottom of the paper reads, "No sign of animal bites on the face or hands. Respect from the rats. Ha!"

Stay up

Keep your body lean

You never know when you're going to have to start running

Learn to duck and cover

I can hear a bullet sliding into a chamber a mile away

At night

I don't sleep

I look out the window and wonder

Who's watching me

Who's waiting out there

Imagine waking up in time

To see someone stab you

I knew a guy. Everyone I know disliked him but tolerated him because he was too pathetic to waste much energy on. He was a wiseass, not afraid to get in the face of big guys and try to piss them off. He was one of those guys with the big self-hatred thing going. You know the type. Funny as hell, but you knew he was dying inside all the time. It's one of the things that made him so hilarious. He always was burning lean tissue. He was always intense. The way one of those little dogs is always intense. The fact that he didn't give a fuck impressed no one. It just scared and alienated everyone around him. He was the kind of guy you didn't want to hang out with because you knew that eventually he would lead you into something that you didn't want to deal with and you knew that he sure wasn't going to be able to back it up. I felt sorry for him because I knew where it all came from. If you had any kind of insight, you knew that you had a little of that in yourself. Not as much as he did though. One night someone broke into his place while he was asleep and beat him to death with a baseball bat. Did more than just kill him, smashed his skull apart. Whoever did it had worked on him for a while. It was personal. He wasn't funny anymore.

It gets sicker and more unbelievable every day

I never thought I would see a time when life imitates the movies

Now you can have a MDE

Michael Douglas Experience

How about the guy who took some potshots at the White House?

How fulfilling it must have been

To think that up in his kitchen

Buy the guns and drive to DC

Walk up to the front of the White House

Marvel that it looks just like he had pictured it

Just like he saw it on TV

And then let loose and watch the white plaster fly

Most of us never get to realize a vision one tenth that intense

Hell of an incentive to get up off the couch and get moving

The best part of the coverage

Was the WH officials downplaying the seriousness of the event

I guess it doesn't look good to get all upset

Over the fact that any random psycho

Or mere mortal citizen

Can do this any time

The way the woman on the screen talked about it was hilarious

"The White House is the People's house. It would be a shame to have to close it off. People like to visit here because they know it is *their* house." When have you ever looked at the White House and thought that? Five minutes away in Southeast DC amidst the project housing, I bet there's not one soul there who thinks they have anything to do with that house. Maybe a distant relative cleans it but other than that..... come on.

Play the cartoon endlessly

Please Mr. Disney

Make another movie with cute animals that talk

Make me almost cry about a lion king

Because I feel like blowing my brains out

I want to choke my woman when she touches me

Make the dreams stop

Take the pollution out of my mind

Take the guns out of my dreams

Take the skin off my face

Take the....

Signal interrupted by intense static

We lost him....

I lost you

Did you lose me?

Turn me off dead man

Turn me off dead

Turn me off

END OF ROUND ONE!

PREPARE YOURSELF FOR

MILITIA MAN!!!

FEAR

The Man was a boy once. There is a room. Square. A bed, a table and a chair. A single bulb hangs from the ceiling. A man sits in the chair. A naked woman walks into the room. He takes his clothes off and they have violent sex on the bed. She remains passive and wordless for the length of the act. After the man ejaculates, he takes a large knife from under the bed and stabs her several times in the face, ribs and stomach. He stops when he is out of breath. He gets up and puts his clothes back on. Moments later, the man's father walks into the room with a baseball bat. He hands the bat to the man. The man bludgeons the father for several minutes. The father's brains are all over the floor. The man drags the father's body into the corner. The man's mother walks into the room. She hands the man a gun. He shoots her in the face until the gun runs out of bullets. He drags the body into the corner and sits back down in the chair. It starts again in ten minutes.

Soundtrack for the rest of my life. Summer. Heat and damp, night and day. You can't escape it. You sleep and sweat, you fuck and sweat, you think and sweat. The smell of your two bodies fills the air in the room and the moisture holds it and makes you relive it over and over breath after breath. You die without going anywhere. Stomachs slick and rubbing together. Cum and sweat. Wet hot greasy necks trying to break themselves. All the sucking and smacking sounds. The sound of teeth clicking. Makes me think of what it would sound like to hack a human to pieces. Stabbing the chest cavity. The sucking wet sounds it would make as you stabbed. The heat works on your brain. You're living in a fucking monkey house. The heat bends everything. The heat beats down with lead gloves. You understand the monster.

Gunshots as poetry. The man in the sedan cuts off the cab driver. The cab driver beeps his horn and the sedan's window unrolls and a pudgy hand comes out and limply flips off the cab driver. The cab driver gets out of the cab, his face streaming with sweat. He tries to get the man in the sedan to come out of the car so he can beat him up right there on the median strip. There's nowhere for the sedan to go. There was an accident at the intersection and traffic is at a total standstill. The cab driver stands outside the sedan looking down at the man inside. The man is looking straight through the windshield trying to ignore him. The cab driver's hand turns into a solid rock and he starts to punch the sedan's window with steady pounding thunder. After a dozen blows or so, the window splinters and cracks. Blood streams from the cab driver's knuckles. The man in the sedan looks like he just ate a big plate of his own shit. The cab driver looks at the small crowd that has gathered to watch the confrontation. He looks in at the man again and slowly goes to his cab, gets in and waits for the traffic to clear.

Animal act. I can't talk to you. When you call me, my throat starts to close. You ask me what's wrong with my voice and I tell you that I'm a little tired hoping that will mask the fact that I want to slam the phone down and rip the cord out so it will never ring again. I don't want to go into the parts about wanting to see myself dead and the part where I wake up almost every night now in a total panic. Telling you doesn't do a damn thing for me. If I did tell you, you would try to say something to make me feel better and that would just make me tell you to shut the fuck up you stupid bitch what the fuck do you know about me. You would say something about wanting to touch me and that would make it worse. It's the thought of someone touching me that makes me want to hack their arms off so they won't try to reach out to me ever again. I wake up in dread. I think I'll choke one of these nights. All I can think about is Death. In the middle of the night I fear it. I really do. I don't want to fuck you because you're a human being. You've got the human stink all over you. When I fuck, I know that I'm just following her fucked up footsteps. I'm just hopping in the grave with her. I try to form words to fool you into thinking that I'm fine so you'll stop talking to me. But really, all I want to do is scream and break things and kill.

The sidewalk spits in your face. It occurs to me now that I have never been the same after you left me. I feel humiliated and empty. I feel like a fool. Somehow I think I should have seen it coming. I have been with other women since you and it's been such a waste of time. I used to laugh at people who said that when their hearts were broken they had a hard time finding someone they could be with. I never thought that would never happen to me. I had contempt for anyone who ever cried or wasted time lamenting over a relationship gone bad. I don't laugh anymore because I would only be laughing at myself. The whole thing has had a bad and long lasting effect on me. I like to spend more time alone than ever before. I have immediate dislike for anyone who says they like me. I reject people's advances with a knee jerk speed that's disturbing. And if you were to call me right now and tell me that you want me back, I would tell you to go fuck yourself. Not because I hate you but because I don't want anyone to be close to me anymore, not even you.

Larry über alles. Movie Idea: Larry is 32 years old and works at an office in a low-level position. He is overweight and has a low self opinion. He lives alone and doesn't do much on the week-ends besides watch television. When he watches, he doesn't pay attention to the show, he just passes time. One day at work he hits upon the idea that he should kill himself. He goes out and buys a handgun. He sits with the gun at home looking at it, pulling the trigger down on empty chambers. He looks over all the bullets in the box that he bought. He picks one. This will be the one that he kills himself with. He carries it around with him. He puts it on his desk during the day and talks to it occasionally. For the first time in his life, he feels alive now that he has plans to end his life. For the first time his life has direction. It occurs to him that he better look good when he goes out. He signs up at a gym and starts to work out in earnest. As the months go by, we see Larry lose body fat and become more muscular. He starts to cultivate a healthy amount of self-respect and people around him start to notice. Women smile at him when before, they never noticed him. All the while he talks to the bullet, which is now shined to perfection. He flips it in his hand when he talks to people. Someone asks him about it and he tells them it's his lucky charm. Months go by and Larry is looking good. He takes his lucky charm and shoots himself in the head with it and leaves a good looking corpse from the neck down. The end.

The great explorer broke down and abandoned his search. Humanity had spat in his face too many times. He turned it around and killed three. Moments before the gas, we hear his anti-speech. My mother's mother drank herself to death. It all comes running out of me, this black water. I see her on the floor, the way they found her days later. She had started to decompose. Her body in a frozen crawl, turning black, fluid leaking through the cloth of her nightgown into the floorboards. From the position of her body, it looked like she was trying to get to the phone. My mother's father drank himself to death. He died down in the cellar. He lived alone. By the time his body was found, he had exploded. You never escape me. I have you with me forever. You will never escape my eyes. You will never escape my voice. I have you in my spell for the rest of your life. You will never forget the way I speak to you. I can see the room the way I want it now. The two of them are on the floor. The two corpses, oozing and putrescent. My mother is on the couch looking at them and crying. Her tears are made out of wood and coal. She has never had a real feeling in her life. She was never really alive. She sees everything through the eyes of a dead thing that has never seen the light of day. She sits on the couch looking at the dead bodies, the two dead drunks. She thinks. *They used to fuck and I came from this. I came from this filth.* She sees what she is now. She wants something to take her mind off of herself. She looks around the room for a man to fuck. She throws a leg over the body of her father and attempts to have sex with it. I come into the room and see them all on the floor. I kick them. Mouthfuls of black blood come flying out of my mother's mouth. While in my holding cell, I have thought of nailing her hand to the floor and kicking her until she exploded. So many times I have killed her for all the times that she made me feel dead like her. I come from death. I come from darkness. I am the most alive and brightest burning thing there is. To you, I am a superstar. I overcome myself by incinerating myself. Her bloodsucking vomiting body is convulsing under the weight of my vision. You will never forget my voice. Ok, I'm ready. Let's do it.

Now it can be told. The man goes to the television station and waits in the parking lot for Jerry Rivers, the television talk show host, to get off work. Eventually Rivers comes outside and starts walking to a sports car. The man walks stiffly towards him and does his best to impersonate a harmless, starstruck fan. The man asks for an autograph. While Rivers is signing a piece of paper, the man pulls out a length of pipe and bashes him in the head as hard as he can. Rivers falls to the ground and starts convulsing in mute stupid animal panic. The man kicks Rivers' head until his brains and eyes come out. You should have a piece of wire tied around your dick and be lead out into traffic and then shot at a red light. Put that in your book. Go fuck yourself. Go march in a parade. I'll be the one in the crowd who opens up on all of you with a machine gun. I won't miss. After I get to you, you will only be recognizable by your dental records.

Friend. You can fake them out so easily. You can lie with a smile and they'll tell their friends that you were so cool when they met you. You can almost make the words come out of their mouths. You want to compliment them and ask them the answer to easy questions so they'll feel that you are stupid and they are smart. It's a great way to make someone give you what you want. Make them think that they're in control. All the while you're laughing behind your eyes calling them every name in the book. Be careful though. You don't want to come off as patronizing. You see those shitheads on television talk shows do it. I saw some piece of shit talking to this very corny actor whose name I won't mention because I don't want him to sue me, resulting in him getting his knee caps broken. Anyway, I wondered what in the hell you could say to this guy that would be a compliment and also be true? "I think your wife's mustache is funny enough but tell her not to take her clothes off in films anymore. It puts me off my food." No, this is national television. The ass kisser complimented the guy on his new piece of shit movie that he did and got him to open up and say the stupidest shit. Another way to make people work for you: agree with everything they say. Don't let them catch on of course. They will tell others how cool you are and how you two really "connected." People are such suckers. That's how serial killers get away with so much shit. A guy pulls up in a van and tells a girl to get in and go for a ride. She gets in and the guy rapes her and throws the body off a cliff and drives home. Easy. The pigs found her a year later with the icepick still in her head. Basically, you want to make a person feel good. When they feel good, they think that they're powerful. When they're under that delusion, play 'em like a fucking video game. Hack them up, pull their teeth out, drive them to tears, make them fall in love with you, just for something to do. When they love you, then you get them to take out all the money in their bank accounts and give it to you. Then you tie them to a chair in their living room, cover them with gasoline and torch them. Keep telling them that they're great and in charge of their lives. It's what I did to my parole officer and it worked out fine. More later. Bye!

Weapon. Don't tell me that you love me. I'll start laughing in your face. You don't want to make me angry. Shut your fake ass mouth and get the fuck out of my face before I hurt you. I don't want you to love me. Don't feed the bullshit machine, there's already enough in it. You think that no one can live without love? You're wrong. You have inflicted enough damage into me. I'm still trying to get the glass out of my guts. It's unbelievable to me that I haven't killed you yet. It's because of you that I won't hesitate to take affection and use it against the one giving it. You should see me in action. I should have a fucking sign around my neck. *Don't pet the animal.* I can't help myself. When a woman tells me that she likes me, I hate her immediately and only want to fuck her and leave. I'm at the point now where I don't even want to fuck them. I just want to scream at them to get the fuck away from me. So next time you see me, don't say a fucking word and just keep walking.

Cancerous fire-breathing bitch. In the first scene, he comes home from school and finds his mother in the living room standing rigidly with her hands on her hips. She opens her mouth to speak but her mouth keeps opening well past the normal width. She exhales and at first all you hear is the sound of someone getting their skin torn off their back. Her throat expands, wide, wider. A fully developed fetus complete with afterbirth comes shooting out and lands a few feet away from the boy. She wipes her mouth off and lights a cigarette and kicks the fetus. She starts to speak; it sounds like a dozen beer bottles caught in a lawnmower. "Your fucking father is late again with his fucking check! I fucking hate him. He ruined my life. Look at me. Do I look like a mother to you? Jesus fucking Christ... oh god damn it." She bends over and wretches. A large steaming mass of blood and tissue falls from her mouth onto her shoes. She looks up at him, "I hate you. I fucking hate you so much!" There is no second scene.

Could it be I'm falling in love? I'm in a hotel room on the second floor. It's 6:04 a.m. I am awakened by the sound of the sliding glass door to the balcony being forced open. I quickly exit the bed and pick up a ten pound barbell weight from the floor. The door slides open slowly. I am waiting with the iron plate. The intruder comes in—I bash the intruder as hard as I can in the head. I turn on the light. It's a man—Caucasoid, medium build. He's dead. I pick up the body and throw it off the balcony as far as I can. The body falls onto the sidewalk. I wipe off the handle of the door so his fingerprints are no longer there. I wash the barbell plate off in the tub. In the morning a policeman comes to the door asking if I heard anything strange last night. I tell him no and show him the ear plugs that I sleep with. He tells me that they found a body on the parking lot and they're looking for leads to see if anyone might have seen who dumped it. He thanks me for my time and leaves. It's great. The lady behind the checkout desk says the cops think that the stiff got dropped off by a car in the middle of the night. She says that kind of thing happens out in these parts. I got to kill somebody and get away with it. I feel great. I mean, wouldn't you? You're like me. You know how many times you've fantasized about killing someone and getting away with it clean. You've always wondered what it would be like to kill somebody. In your mind you've killed so many times it's not funny. You've killed your parents, lovers, bosses, etc. You know that if you ever did, you would feel like the most powerful person in the world. I bet you've come up with ways to do it and not get caught. That's the only thing that stops you—fear of getting caught and doing time. That and guilt of course. I feel fine. I don't care about human life. You're all strangers to me. You're all *its* and *them*. Fucking insects, that's all you are.

Kicking the pigskin. I saw the pig in his car. I was crossing the parking lot. There was no other way I could go. The sidewalk was blocked by construction. I don't want to walk by a pig car with a pig in it. You never know what could happen. Pigs are weak and they lash out. I walked by the pig car as quickly as I could. I tried not to look in at the pig but I had to so I would know if I had to run. I wish I didn't look. There was some boy sucking on the pig's dick. I shot the pig in his mouth. I will never forget look on that kid's face when he looked up at me from the pig's lap. His face was covered with brains and cum. It was then that I recognized him. The little shit lives three doors down from me!

Urban contemporary blues. I called and called. She never picked up the phone. All I would get was her answering machine. I would leave thirty minute messages telling her how much I loved her and missed her and would she please come back to me. The days passed like glass splinters under my skin. I couldn't understand for the life of me why she wouldn't at least talk to me. She had dropped me so abruptly. She had never told me why she had started going out with this other guy. I thought things were going so well. I stopped calling her. A few months went by and I thought I had it beat. You will call me a damn fool for what I did next. In a fit of romantic rage, I cut off my ear and sent it to her. I figured that she would at least call me or something. Maybe she would see that I was the one who truly loved her, because you know, I did. Do you know how hard it is to cut off a human ear? It's hard as shit. I had to do it in the mirror. I nearly chickened out halfway through. The pain was beyond belief. So yeah, I sent her my ear in the mail, first class. A week later, I got a slip in the door that said I had a parcel waiting for me at the post office. I went and got it. It was my ear. The jiffy envelope had a sticker on it that said: *Return to sender – No longer at this address – Unable to forward.*

War on our shores. I want impress you in the hope that you might trust me. I want your trust more than anything in the world, more than I want to live. I run my hands up and down your beautiful body. You show me all the scars that your father put on you. All the cigarette burns and bite marks. There's so many of them. You've been hurt so many times. I touch the necklace of human teeth that hangs around your neck. The teeth are yours. He pulled them out of your head with pliers in the basement every Sunday until you had no more left. You can't stop feeling his hands on you. You thought the scar tissue would dull the pain but it didn't. I know you could not possibly have killed him enough times in your mind to have him dead in your dreams forever. I know this. I feel the same way. I will be the one who will always love you no matter where you are. I will be the one you will remember as the only one who didn't bring you pain. I take you to a large walk-in freezer. I take you on a tour of the hundreds of corpses hung up on hooks—all of them my mother and father. Killed so many times, so many different ways. You see many similarities. The father with the hook through the neck, face beaten to an unrecognizable mess, entrails. Killed so many times. Trying to take the pain away. Blinded by scar tissue. Aren't we all. I look at you to see if I can detect anything in your eyes. You look at me and I can see that you trust me. You see that I'll never hurt you. We drop to the ground and fuck on the floor under the slowly swaying feet of hundreds of broken knuckled aborted screams. Your scars make you look better. I know you're real.

Flame on! A pig got torched on Lincoln Blvd. Cuffed to a cement light pole and lit on fire. Funniest thing. That fucking arrogant pig was giving me shit all the way up until I lit the match and threw it on his pointy head. "You're in shit city, asshole!" Etc. The pig was vainly attempting to affect what is called "Command Presence". CP is being able to take total control of a situation immediately. You see it when pigs stop people for running red lights and parking violations and shit. They make it sound like they're invading Poland or something. It's all acting. I don't take pig talk lightly but I take it for what it is. So imagine what the fuck that looks like when the pig lights up the night. Screaming, and straining against the cuffs, trying to suck his dick so he could have a man in his mouth one last time. His uniform burns off except the belt. Appropriate too, as a lot of cops leave their belts on when they fuck each other in high school parking lots. How did I get the pig's cuffs? Pigs are stupid and go for most lines. You can take one to the top of a tall building and tell him that there's a stiff dick and a Mexican to beat up at the bottom and they'll jump down there as fast as they can. Why does this shit surprise you? You have this world around you and you still insist that you're different than the rest. You act like you're shocked but inside you wish for more murder, more catastrophe. If they could have executions of Death Row inmates on pay-per-view, it would be the biggest money maker going. The country's money problem would be over in a matter of months. Why do I do this? Why am I burning? Why do I pull fire from the sky? Why am I a living explosion? I will never stop. It will come like a volcano. At the end of the line, the questions will all be theirs. I'll leave with ashes on my face and my hands empty.

Fat loudmouthed has-been no one wants to fuck you. The thought of prison keeps you safe from me. So many times I've looked at you and imagined snapping your neck or just leaning over the counter and stabbing you in the throat as you ring up my food, you piece of shit. I think about it all the time. You're safe though because the thought of prison freaks me out. The idea of going to prison for the rest of my life because all I did was kill you makes me sick. I would want to dig you up and kill you again if that was possible. Take your corpse and bash it with a hammer in front of your grieving parents just to hear them scream in horror. That's the only thing that keeps the streets in my neighborhood safe. I take it out anyway I can. I kick animals any chance I get. I crank call the parents of old girlfriends telling them that I have the bitch in my cellar and I'm killing her slowly with tools. Pulling her eyes out with pliers, that kind of shit. When they scream, I tell them to shut the fuck up. The mothers always believe me. I hang up and punch the wall and imagine her face. I'm always calm when I see you though. You never see this side. You never will. I can look right at you and make you think that I am an oasis of understanding and kindness. Looking at your believing eyes and tender expression makes me want to spit on you. You should be killed all the time. When one of you is nice to me, all I see is a throat to be cut. It makes me hate you. I can barely restrain myself from killing you. When you try to touch me, I want to vomit. It makes me want to break your arm. Prison keeps me from killing you. I can't live in this world. I think I was put here just to burn. Everything hurts. Daylight, voices, the stench of life. It's all repulsive. The thought of spending the rest of it in a human zoo keeps me grinding my teeth. If I thought I could get away with it, I would. I would kill all the time. Every chance I got. Men, women, makes no difference. I don't care if I know them or not. Any living human besides myself will do. It's the only way to ease the pain. I know that I will not be able to fight off this urge forever. It's too fucking strong inside me. When I kill, there will be no guns used. It will be all knives and blunt instruments. How good would that feel, to work someone over with a pipe until the body has no bones that are whole? You could really sleep well after that. Knifing someone until you had no more strength. Leave the bodies in places that are heavily populated. Leave a body hanging nude and battered from a basketball rim. I'll never get caught. I'll never stop once I've started. I know it will be too good.

Human video shithole machine, get another nose job. You think you're on your way but you're only on their way. You're playing your game but really you're playing their game. You want the house on the hill. They move out the old fool and throw in the new meat. The masters own the game and they move you into the well-worn slot. They feed themselves on your blood. They stay young. You get worked. Look at your fucked up face and tell me I'm wrong. I see you running around making all your phone calls thinking you're such a fucking mover. If you could see yourself, you might puke. You're fast talking and pathetic. It's funny watching you do your routine. Hanging up the phone and laughing about the suit you think you just stiffed when you need him to exist and he needs you like he needs another bill in the mail. You don't see that you're just another in a long line of fuckheads who come up to the plate and take a swing. The big house on the hill looms large in your mind but you're still under lock and key. You'll always work for the man you say you hate. You will always kiss his ass because it's all you know how to do. People like you get used until there's nothing left and all the while you think you're in paradise. You're weak and disgusting but you never get in my way.

All my children are broken bones. I can close my eyes and see myself in a dirty room. I can smell my mother's anger. I can smell all the men who walked through the place. I can hear the screams of the years of fear. I can smell the leather as it slammed into my skin. The scars talk to me. All I can do now is exhale, inhale, vent the rage. I wonder if real life has started yet. Is this it? Is the killing wound the only wound to hatch from? Can I reinvent myself in blood and stone? Burn muscle into forged fury? Once a veteran always a veteran. Shock to shock. There is a dark room always ready to receive. Always a room on the highway that has my name on it. Always a fucked up memory to cause more brain cancer. Some people will never stop. They have no control over the rolling tragedy that is their lives. A walking accident that loves to happen. Revenge is not the operative. It's caged animal sickness, that's all.

Choking hands. He had one of those typical piece of shit days. The grind always. At least this time he had the guts to stay away from the bar and not drive home to the wife and kid drunk. He got home and immediately everything pissed him off. Sometimes the way his wife looked at him made him want to kill himself. The way she all of a sudden appeared like a total stranger. The vacancy in her eyes, it was bad. He took his son's favorite plastic mug, the one with the picture of Magic Johnson, and threw it into the trash. He felt better but not much.

You and your glycerin tears. You're a TV actor and all of a sudden the still life of your fucked up world of desperate AA meetings and panicked last chance lunges at Christ's punk ass salvation are shook loose when reality comes crashing in. Your son is dead. Shot in the face. I wish it was you instead. You couldn't even make it to the funeral. You're a living piece of shit. Why couldn't it have been you? I wouldn't have lost a minute of sleep. It was great to see you in your moments of pain. You looked so good for the camera, so well rehearsed. I swear I saw you do that on Channel 7 once. Am I being too mean, shithead? I'm not sorry. Your weakness is so disgusting and I have a tendency to attack that which I don't respect so I'm attacking you. It's your only son and all you can do is try to look good and manage to be late for every meeting while your relatives talk over all the boring, less glamorous details involved with dealing with your son's refrigerated corpse. You seemed more interested in your son's material things than you were in him. What are you going to do? Sell his clothes? You and your designer tennis suits and your arrogant bullshit. I heard you have a history of suicide on your side of the family. I am hoping you're going to do it on New Year's. That would be great to hear about how you shot yourself in the face underneath your fake ass Christmas tree. Should I just stop right here and put my arms around you and tell you that it's all going to be alright? Should I? Hey fuck you. The more I think about you and your fucked up little friend that you brought everywhere with you, the more I want to make your life miserable in hopes that you'll kill yourself. Yes, I'd like to help you. I will concentrate all my best blow-my-brains-out thoughts over to you every day and if the wind is just right, you'll pick up on the signal and check out. Your friends at the wake—fake grief and studio tans. The one ugly, leather-faced bitch who should have kept her sagging breasts covered up was asking me what my sign was. Remember a couple of summers ago, when you kept trying to get me to go on those stupid tabloid TV shows with you? I said no and it really burned you. I saw the footage of you on Hard Copy walking to your son's grave with the soft focus and the bullshit music soundtrack. Was it hard to get the cemetery to let you get the film crew inside the lot? Did you have to do a few takes to get the walk right? Who did your make-up? Do you remember you went on the Joan Rivers Show and talked all that shit about me? I know someone who was at one of your auditions a few weeks ago. Apparently you were really bad and you finally apologized and told them that you were hungover. I guess you fell off the wagon. I wish you would jump off the top of a forty story building. You're such a fuck up.

Now all you have is your fake friends who will never be there for you when you need them because they're not there for anyone ever, not even themselves. You can't even help yourself. You're the most pathetic person I know.

Sell the tourists human ears. Watch a man get his spine ripped out every day for 30 years. A man alone in his room thinking about killing someone and then wishing he wasn't so lonely. He has no idea that his brain is in hundreds of pieces underneath his scalp. He vomits his bone marrow whenever he speaks. He cuts himself on words. Nothing helps him from destroying himself. This man needs no drugs or alcohol to ruin himself. All he needs is life itself. The fact that he has a mother somewhere is horror enough. The fact that he has touched a woman and still has the skin on his back to prove it is bad enough. Anything that he has to feel is too much to deal with. He lives in the world that does not feel, that does not touch. At night he dreams of not being real. He dreams of getting out of his skin so he can have a breath that's not like breathing in the sorrow of night. The black air of madness. I am falling through the night. I see things out of the corners of my eyes. My spine crawls across the floor and wraps itself around my feet. Nothing gets to me anymore. It's all horrible. I'm free.

Load the guns. Repeat, "They're just ants at the picnic." Walk into the dance with both barrels blazing. When I go to the store and have to walk around all the whores and drug dealers who block the sidewalk, I always wish one of the ones who didn't have a gun would talk some shit so I could mutilate him. I'm not talking about a run-of-the-mill ass-kicking. I'm talking about taking eyes out and breaking joints and smashing windpipes. It would be good to do that to a Hollywood neon shitboy and then hang him from a stop sign to let the rest know what happens to them when they open their dogshit mouths to the wrong person. Look. I see it. You can go to all the movies and watch all the television you want. I am the end of all time. I'm not hooked up to the machine. I don't care about being labeled a misogynist, misanthropic hate addict. I don't give a fuck if some human organism calls me politically incorrect. I like the idea of people getting killed in parking lots. I stab every person who passes me. In my mind, I stab them in the face with a fucking knife. If I thought I could get away with it, I would skin you alive. I only fear prison if I get caught killing one of you humans. I hate you all. I don't know anyone. I am the enemy of humans. I am that which spits in the face of humanity.

Boots on, trousers down. Onwards to victory. Hello? Yeah man. Look man, your daughter is dead. She got burned on a drug deal and she got wasted. Don't ask me my name, man. Look, it's not me who did it so don't be getting all harsh on me. I loved her, man. She was my old lady and shit. We left her in a warehouse on 3rd and Kent downtown. You should get her picked up man, she's been there a few days. If you don't pick her up soon, the dogs will eat her. Yeah, it's pretty fucked. I've seen it before. We didn't know where to find you. I feel bad about it man. Don't come looking, you know what I mean? Cool. Later, man.

If we didn't act our ages and acted our bank accounts instead, I'd be Father Time and you'd be teething. She belted him right in the mouth. It felt good. It had been building up all week. She would come home from work and there he was, sitting with the baby and listening to some shitty punk rock music. She had no words for him. All she could do was hit. The baby would cry and she would yell and he would scream and cry and the neighbors on all four sides would knock or kick the wall, floor and ceiling. She didn't care. They would both yell at the neighbors to shut up. It was usually the thing that would get the fight to stop though. He would go see to the baby as she was walking to the box to get a beer. She had planned on being an artist.

You want to be an actress so you figure you'll work on your technique by dancing naked in front of a bunch of idiots for seven years? I watched her shoot up in the bathroom. We had just finished fucking. I thought she was in the kitchen so I went to the toilet and she was in there with the door open. I just looked at her. She looked up at me and said hi and went back to shooting the dope into her foot. I didn't know she did that shit. I couldn't tell when we were fucking. I wondered how long she had been doing that shit but I was afraid to ask. I don't know why I was afraid, I just was. She finished and leaned back against the wall and closed her eyes. I asked her if she was alright. She didn't say anything. She waved me away and I left the fucking place. She had said earlier that she had a boyfriend who was in jail and some of his friends would check up on her from time to time. I don't know what the hell I even went to her place for. I guess I was lonely. She had a hard beauty that I hadn't ever seen in a woman. I thought about her for days afterwards. I never saw her again. I heard that she dumped the guy and married some Marine and the two of them moved to North Carolina. People get caught here on Earth. We do the time and shit happens. I end up, you end up. Don't try to make any big sense of it. That's the first mistake. The more you try to figure it out, the more it fucks you up. I don't know what the second mistake is.

The room smells like vomit these days. She throws up every morning. She coughs and hacks into the bowl. Her breasts scrape the rim. She wipes her mouth off with a washcloth and gets ready for work. The pigs put the boy in the back of the car. The pigs shoved him in the back without trying to get his head under the roof. I saw them smash his head against the sides of the door like the way old Ma rings the triangle at dinner time when it's time to, "Come and git it!" I was standing there with a bunch of other people. The club owner had locked us inside so watching was all we could do. I felt like an asshole standing in the window watching this guy get worked over but there's only so much you can do without modern firearms. Which leads me to the conclusion that life would be a lot more bearable if I had access to a RPG or a mortar. Hell, how about missiles, tanks? Thinking about it, I would have to put my money on that good old RPG. A good tool for traffic jams. Fuck it, someone should have shot that pig in the ass while he was fucking with that guy. These shitheads never get what they really need.

All we are is angel dust in the wound. Rats chewed the hands, lips, and nose off a three month-old girl in the apartment building across the street from me. The mother was on PCP and had her head in the stove trying to kill herself. God angel devil lover. In my house. Make it hot and kill it quick.

A black guy and a Korean guy, arms around each other watching a white guy hang by the neck. United colors of we'll-do-anything-to-sell-these-fucking-clothes-to-you-morons. He shot the guy. Big fucking deal. I saw the whole thing while I was walking back from doing the laundry. The guy just fell over. The gun didn't make much noise. The guy who shot him ran away and no one went after him, the guy had a gun! I felt absolutely nothing. I think I've been living in this city too long. I work. I hate it but I do it. What the fuck else am I going to do? Rob a bank? I hate my job. I hate my life so what else is new? I've got ten minutes until I have to go to work. Ten whole minutes to myself. What should I do with my big ten minutes? I might as well go into work early. Fuck it.

What about a gaaaaaaaaaaay GI Joe doll? I got your letter today. I should start by saying that I don't hate you. I don't have any problems with you, or that is to say that I will not accept you as the blame for my state of being. In the last few years it has been very difficult for me to get by without bad depression. I have been doing a lot of thinking as to the root of all the bullshit that I put myself through. I ask myself why I do all this music and writing bullshit. I know why I do it all. I am trying to get out all the rage that I have. Do you know where that rage comes from? It comes from the way I was raised. I have a rage in me that dries my bone marrow, it goes so deep. All I can do now is make my rent money and eat year after year. It is up to me to get myself better. I know I was a horrible person growing up. I was never good at school, sports. I was a disappointment on all levels. I am only good at one thing: that is the taking of and dispensing pain. I know humiliation, that's why I work so hard. No one will ever walk on me again. I command respect through intimidation and the fact that I will persist after all the rest have given up. My capacity for taking pain is what I am most proud of. It's all I know at this point. I should have died when I was born. I have no happy memories of childhood. I know you did the best you could and I have no regrets and I appreciate all you did for me and I know you did your best and I know you gave up a part of your life to raise me. I know there were things you would have done differently if you didn't have me. I also know that I didn't ask to be born. It is hard for me to deal with women past a business level. The thought of intimacy is repulsive and out of the question. I learned about sex by walking down the hall and seeing you and some guy. One of them once told me once how good you are in bed. Do you have an idea what kind of shit that does to a freaked out little boy? To me, every woman is a bitch. I make sure I hurt every one of them mentally when I have sex with them. I like the mental pain I cause them more than I like the sex I have with them. I do my best to feel legitimate and that I deserve a life. It is an ongoing struggle. So in the last two years I have had difficulty in dealing with you. This is no fault of yours. I hope that someday that I can be your friend. I don't mean to make this a problem. It is a full-time thing for me to maintain. I have bad problems with depression. It's like a plague. It makes me want to either kill someone or kill myself. It sometimes ends with me beating some guy up. I never would take my fists to a female. I think you are a good person and I know that you want to do good things. The problem with you and me not connecting is a problem that comes from my end. I can't help how I feel though. I wish I didn't feel like this. I would of rather have had a normal life. Not the strange one that I have now. I feel more in common with a guy who murders a lot of people than I do with anyone in my world. So that's it. My life is fucked. You wanted to know what was going on with me and I told you the best I could.

I guess you all were too young for EST. Lucky. I am chained to a steel bedpost. Every few hours my mother comes in and beats me and then she sends in one of her boyfriends to kiss me and hit me with his belt. They always tell me that they love me. I do this alone in my room. I can do it anytime I want. Then I want to go to her house and beat her sleeping body until the brains start coming out. I can smell it all now because that's how it's going to be. It's going to be a smell thing. Blood, shit and brains. Nothing smells like human brains. It's a thick sweet smell. It will drive you insane.

You should have killed me when you had the chance. You fucking missed me twice. Fuck you. I was walking up Hollywood Blvd. I saw a girl sitting on the ground outside of the Chinese Theater. She motioned for me to come over. She wanted to know if I would buy some sunglasses off her for a dollar so she could get money to go to Las Vegas. I asked her why she was asking for a dollar if she was planning such a long trip. She said, "I'm a Hollywood fuckup," and that she was trying to get her shit together. I could tell by her eyes that she was a junkie. She was looking pretty bad. I asked her if she wanted to get high. She said that she was trying to get off the shit but it was hard and she would really dig getting high right now because she had been puking all day. I told her to come with me and she could suck my dick and I'd give her twenty bucks. She got up and we went to a parking garage near my place. I took her around the back to the fire exit that's never watched and never locked and we went in and up the stairs to the second level. I was amazed at how trusting she was. She asked me if I wanted to score with her. She said that she would come over and we could party at my place after we got the shit. I told her that was cool. I told her, "I love to party," to see if I could make her laugh. She looked at me and said that I looked like it. We got up to the second level and I walked her to the corner behind the fucked up van that had been sitting there all summer. She got down on her knees and started trying to undo my belt buckle. I stood her up and hit her in the face as hard as I could. She fell on the ground and put her hands on her head. I kicked her until I was barely able to breathe. I treat humans like what they are—garbage.

It's easy to play god trips on your head. They are talking a bunch of shit late into the early morning hours. I can hear them from my room. They're sitting in a car outside. I can feel their heat. I can taste the food they ate on their spent breath as it comes out of their mouths. I can sense them totally. I could kill them with my eyes closed but I had them open the whole time I clubbed the man to death. He was so easy. I went outside and kicked the side the bitch was sitting on and of course the guy came out and asked me if I had a problem. This made me laugh. There is a big difference between me and that guy. The difference is that I kill people. I hit him in the face as hard as I could with the bat and killed him with one shot. I clubbed his head until I saw his brains and then ran down the alley and through the back door. My block is so fucked up that no one looks out the windows anymore anyway. The cunt just sat in the car and watched. I got away clean. There's a big difference between you and me. I kill humans. I end their lives and ruin the lives of their families. I don't give a fuck about anyone but myself. I know the meaning of life. It has no meaning. I kill you and it doesn't matter. It's the way I can pass time and respect myself you fuckhead.

There's a lady who knows..... Here's what happened and it's the fucking truth. I was walking from the store. I don't like going out in the day. I can't take the sun. It's not good for me. I don't like all the ugly fucking people looking at me like they do. All I can do is dream of killing them. It would so good to just be able to shoot them like the pieces of shit that they are. Their eyes bugging out, their filthy little kids looking and laughing. I go out at night because there's less people out there to fuck with me. I was walking like I said and this pig car pulls up. I stop. Like what the fuck am I going to do, keep walking and mind my own business like I haven't done anything? Fuck no. I stop because I know that the pig will to cook up some reason to take me to jail if I don't stop. The pig gets out of the car and asks me where I'm going and I tell him that I'm walking to the store and he says that I'm a faggot looking for some dick to suck. He calls me a cocksucking faggot looking for a little meat. He says that he ought to kick the shit out of me right on the spot. I told him I wasn't a faggot. The pig hits me in the stomach and pulls me to the back seat of his car. He puts his gun to my head and tells me to unzip his pants because I'm going to suck his cock right now. I did it. I sucked the pig's cock. What else was I going to do? He had the gun at my head. I was never with a man before, besides some of my mother's boyfriends and my stepbrother but none of that was my idea. He pushed me out of the car and drove off. I went home. I'm going to kill that fucking pig someday. I'm going to find him and waste his pig ass. It's going to be great. I'll make him suck the gun. Yeah, come on pig. Let's see some feeling. Gimmie some soul when you wrap your tongue around that barrel. I hate those big funerals for cops. The ones where the taxpayers shell out too much money so the pigs can shoot guns and make people think that the dead piece of shit was worth the time of day. They should have the funerals at my house. We could party and drink and laugh and play videos of me shooting the pig over and over. Tie up the pig's boyfriend and mother and make them watch it until they pass out and then kill them. If the pig happened to be married to a woman, then I'll have more fun. I'll follow her around for a few days and get her habits down and then I'll take her out. I'll put a leash on the cunt and take her out for a walk. Fucking pig slut. Come. Heel. Water the flowers with your piss, you fucking bag of shit. You pig fucker. Shoot her in the jaw with a .22 and leave her so she'll be disfigured but not dead. Fuck you, pig. I'm going to kill you.

Sorry, but I'm the REAL voice of the Village. Ha ha. Ho ho. I never wanted you. At night I prayed that you would die inside me. I used to hit you by running into tables as hard as I could, hoping that you would crack your skull. I drank. Oh God, I drank. I did anything I could to try and kill you while you grew inside me. For nine months I felt like I was full of cancer. I should have killed myself in the ninth month. That would have been master work on my part. I hate you. But still you came out. At first I was happy just to have you out of me. I didn't care what you looked like. The nurse asked me if I wanted to hold you and I said no. I should have strangled you while you were asleep. I never wanted you. I want you to know that and never forget it. You ruined my figure. You ruined my life. I hate you. Forever. How do I have a normal sex life with a fucking kid in the house? You think a man wants to come and fuck me when he knows there's a kid in the next room? How am I supposed to be with a man when I know that at any minute you're going to come into the fucking room asking me to fix some fucking toy. They never come to the house again. That's why I hit you every time one of them left. You ruined my life. I never had a life after you came along. I hate you. I remember when I got my boyfriends to hit you. I got sick of touching you, even though it gave me great pleasure to hear you scream. I liked it better when the man did it to you. I always stood outside the door and listened to them hit you. I was always hoping that one of them would kill you and you would be gone and I wouldn't have to do time. I hate you. Do you know what makes me the maddest? The fact that I did everything I could to kill you and nothing worked. You are the Antichrist. You didn't die. Now I wait for my life to end. There's nothing for me now. I am old and ugly and you could come into this room and kill me now if you wanted to. That's why I keep this gun. I hate you. Tonight is the big night. The gun is in my mouth. I am destroying myself tonight. Tonight is the end of my suffering. No more looking in the mirror and seeing this ugly body. The only thing it ever did was give birth to you. I could have been a model. I could have been a stewardess. I could have been anything. But instead, I became a mother. Only one life. Mine is a life wasted because of you. I hate you.

I know, I know, cultivated misanthropic maladjustment. She told me to come into her room. I went in and asked her what she wanted. She said, "I want to give you a nightmare that will last you for the rest of your life." She took out a pistol from under the pillow of her bed and put the barrel in her mouth and pulled the trigger before I could say anything. Her body flew back and landed in the corner. Now she does it three nights a week. It was years ago but the memory is fresh in my mind. The sound of the gunshot roars in my head for hours like a jet engine. Now I have the gun in my hand. I can't sleep. I keep thinking about that shot. I keep thinking about what I need. It's all coming true. Every night I smell the gun powder and my vomit. I keep telling myself to be strong.

Information. Yesterday the first gunshot came in at 7:36 a.m. No return fire. Pack the gat and spray the suckers that sling the crack. Duck and cover. It's not you yet so don't even think about death. It just gets in the way of the real life movie you got going on my fucking street. This wild west has no nobility. Live in fear of the ones who have the ability to see that life has no price and for this, you pay endlessly. You pay with fear. Disease wears a cape and dons a shining shield. The stats break it down to sheer numbers. Reality has become a fear trip. Something to choke on. One in every three women in America will be raped. This is science friction. I see it from all sides. I see the direction of the infection. The facts are stacked and packed into your head. You need the two hour vacation twelve times a day. Spark the joint and park the car. Look up at the stars. Think about it, you're in the hot seat. You're in a huge shark tank. If you want to beat them, you have to join them somehow. The bad guys kill the bad guys. The bad guys kill the good guys. If you want to survive the bad guys, you have to have to have some bad in you—a lot actually. You have to know what they know. This is high adventure in the great outdoors. I don't know what these people thought was going to happen to them. Too much television, too much bad food, too many magazines. Too much time spent worrying about depressed millionaires getting left by their women. Wondering if the fall season shows will be what they should be. Anyone who wants to help me doesn't. Anyone who wants to kill me might. Anyone who wants to love me better not. People are poisonous. When was the last time you wanted to kill someone? I mean *really* kill someone? Where you planned all the shit out, like what to do with the body and all that. When was the last time you really wanted to live? Do you ever have to remind yourself that you're alive? I'm not a light bringer, I'm not a gunslinger. I'm a reporter from the port of soul. Front line at the abyss. If the abyss fits, wear it. Looking into the monster's mouth. The vet turned cop. Man walks a dozen people down the aisle of a convenience store and shoots them. A girl gets raped in the shower a few times and now tries to kill herself often. She's a good American—she'll get it right. Nothing but the facts. I like the ones that make you choke. The truth is my friend. It keeps me warm at night. The truth is your friend even when it's sending you to prison. Even when it kills you and your fuck partner. There will be some bright nights ahead. You'll get used to the smell of napalm. Pigs eating dead bodies and the gun-toting youths who wear your looted watches and rings will not scare you one bit. Feel the fear. And don't forget to get down.

DUST TO ASHES. ASHES TO DUST. DUST TO ASHES. ASHES TO DUST. DUST TO ASHES. ASHES TO DUST. DUST TO ASHES. ASHES TO DUST. DUST TO ASHES. ASHES TO DUST. DUST TO ASHES. ASHES TO DUST.

NOTHING

The streets are white
The squares in the sidewalk are white
The offices
On-screen sex
War heroes
Movie stars
Presidents
Moonwalkers
The master's quarters
The White House
That which validates
That which permits
What is good and pure
White
All white
A few of the men on dollar bills were slaveowners
Doesn't that tell you everything you need to know?
I'm sorry that we all got pulled in
That we all got our limbs bashed and torn off
Force-fed hate
Rewarded for our outbursts of stupidity
Applauded for our ignorance
Stripped of our humanity
They won
They sure beat you
Look at the street you live on
Look into the eyes of those who pass you
Terrified and defeated
It's all over
And it just keeps happening
The great crash finally losing its speed

It's enough to make you cry for a million years
He got killed because he fucked a white woman
He got killed because he told the truth
I knew it was over when I got beaten up at school
For the color of my skin
I knew that humans were not meant to stay around for too long
Didn't the KKK show that it was temporary?
A black man hanging from a tree
An iron cable around his neck
How could you do that to someone?
How could you live with yourself?
Ask a redneck hangman
Fucking neck stretchers
The history books will never get it right
Words are not ugly enough to describe
The rage will never will stop burning
You can't view the past
And expect future generations to forgive or forget
South Africa
South Central
I forgot where I was for a minute
Everything's blurred
America efficiently defoliates square foreign miles
For much less
Than 400 years of murder
They killed us slowly
Now we're extinct
In a few years we'll be forgotten
It breaks my heart over and over
Breaks my spirit
Just understand that the end began long ago

We got here just in time
Look
All the squares in the sidewalks were already here
The streets were already named
All these strangers have more money than you do
All the good riffs have been taken
And everyone is so scared
Murder is commonplace
I don't even flinch at the gunshots outside my window
I feel lonely without them
Pick a prison, any prison, apartment, house
Bars on the windows
People kill each other for what they want
The climate is constant fear and paranoia
Distrust is a way of life
You are either predator or prey
Inmates repeat the same ritual every day
They dream of getting out someday
Now look at your life
Not much difference if you ask me
So free
After....
The seas have dried out
The trains have come to a shrieking halt
The hounds of the abyss cease to howl
The prisons have closed their doors
The pigs have no one to arrest except themselves
The drugs no longer have an effect
When it's all over
All I'll remember is you
The streets are wide and the rooms are full of strangers

They're nothing like you
No one will ever take your place
I can't believe you're gone sometimes
The sadness is crushing
It destroys me
Looking through all the neon and flashing insanity...
These jungle grids
Cities of urgent Death
Full of monster killers like the one who took you away
I am left here alone without you
It's over with
I pass time
I wait around
I don't want to check out
I have to keep fooling myself to keep going
I see the meaning of life
All the things that I know now
I wish I didn't
I know too much truth
It makes me see the futility
Sometimes I think
My heart was broken before I was born
And I spent all this time
Staggering around
Vainly trying to mend what cannot be mended
My tiny truth
My entire life not even registering a blip on the screen
Like an insect howling in a storm-filled canyon
Somewhere there's a bullet casing
4.10.61 - 12.19.91
No silver lining
Just sorrow

Humanity got shown out for what it was
The ultimate con
From Jesus on down the line
Finally, relentless evolution passed us all
No one's ego could handle it
Alas
And then there was Nothing